NOT QUITE RIGHT FOR US

T0346996

flipped eye publishing
London

Not Quite Right for Us: Forty Writers Speak Volumes

First published in 2021 by flipped eye publishing | www.flippedeye.net

Compilation © 2021 Sharmilla Beezmohun
Copyright for individual works rests with their respective authors © 2021
Jacket design by Inua Ellams | www.phaze05.com

First Edition

A CIP catalogue record for this book is available from the British Library.

Printed and bound in Great Britain.

ISBN-13: 978-1-905233-63-2

Not Quite Right for Us celebrates ten years of Speaking Volumes.
www.speaking-volumes.org.uk

Contents

V travel

VI love

VII yesterday/today

VIII today/tomorrow

Foreword

Not Quite Right — For Us

Over the last decade, the literary organisation Speaking Volumes has earned an enviable reputation for promoting writers, mostly from outside the mainstream, especially from ethnic minorities. It has received plaudits along the way for its live events, both at home and abroad. Its timely intervention has gone some way to providing greater visibility for new and emerging voices. A decade is a significant milestone, and what better way to mark the occasion than an anthology of new writing.

To commission a diverse group of writers active in different genres to produce work around the idea of 'not quite right' or 'not quite right for us' is to cast the net wide. The point of departure could have ontological, cultural, psychological and political dimensions. The resulting trawl is a unique collection of writing – short stories, poetry, essays and memoir – exploring an array of scenarios, ideas, emotions and states of being. It reads like an outstanding edition of a choice literary journal, without the reviews and academic articles.

Among the forty contributors are many established writers like Colin Grant, Tabish Khair, E. Ethelbert Miller, Aminatta Forna, Paul Burston and the doyenne of Caribbean letters, Olive Senior. Representatives from the younger generation include award-winning poet Jay Bernard, Amina Atiq, Fergal Harte, afshan d'souza-lodhi and Laniyuk.

For some of the contributors, 'not quite right for us' raises questions about race, class, sexuality, gender, identity and belonging. Nazneen Khan-Østrem writes about the lure of British pop music in the 1980s and the "dark streak" of fascism in the punk rock movement in 'This is England. But Not for Me'. In 'The Freshie Rocker', afshan d'souza-lodhi reflects on the dilemma, for an Asian girl, of 'assimilation' into British youth culture and fealty to one's own roots. Francesca Beard meditates on the challenges of "navigating the foreign familiar" in her poem 'Alien'. Andy Jackson writes about the quotidian burden of otherness for the disabled.

The brief given to the writers is sufficiently elastic to include everyday interactions that elicit feelings of unease. John Hegley writes a humorous poem, 'The Wrong Clothing', about being inappropriately attired for the school disco. 'The Apocrypha of O', Gaele Sobott's post-apocalyptic tale of an eco-warrior and a seed collector valorises transgressive sexuality. In her story 'Impulse', Aminatta Forna takes us into the fantasised world of a mentally ill woman. Leone Ross's ironic tale of maternal obsession, 'Knot', also looks at the dire mental consequences of a black woman's racial negation.

Naturally, 'not quite right for us' is a familiar phrase heard by writers trying to get their work published, especially those not considered mainstream enough. For writers like Olive Senior, it is "a pivot on which resistance turns". In her essay 'I'm Quite Alright with That', she writes about how, in her fiction and poetry, her speakers resist or reject that notion, as she herself does in the practice of her art. She confesses that, whilst the characters and stories are not her own, "they certainly embody my own lifelong impulse to subvert authority, to challenge fake respectability, to shrug off the gatekeepers of personhood, history and story".

Raman Mundair's 'The Anatomy of Rejection OR The Power of Unbelonging' is as combative as it is eloquent. For her, 'not quite right for us' embodies "Narcissus staring at his own reflection again and again, blind to all the life around him, choosing only himself". She deconstructs the phrase and offers a devastating critique, writing that 'quite' suggests "tantalisingly close", 'right', "the norm" and 'us', "gatekeepers" … and goes on to interrogate various aspects of othering. Like Olive Senior, Mundair regards the phrase as a challenge for writers on the periphery: "It is a moment to step forward and assert our stories louder, to create alternative spaces and platforms …We must affirm and choose ourselves".

Paul Burston raises the question of literariness in his essay 'A Stranger Here Myself'. He wants to know "why should LGBTQ+ writers be obliged to write in any given style?" He asserts that their storytelling styles can be as varied as anyone else, and goes on to say that "sometimes it isn't homophobia or heterosexism you're up against, but just plain snobbery". Having opted for a measure of the autonomy that Olive Senior and Raman Mundair embrace by founding his own literary salon, Polari, and a literary prize, Burston is aware that, in the eyes of others, he too has become a gatekeeper.

This anthology of new writing consisting of insightful memoir, a variety of poetic styles and musings, thoughtful essays and exceptional short stories is a refreshing, engaging read. *Not Quite Right for Us*, to paraphrase Olive Senior, is quite alright for me.

Linton Kwesi Johnson
London, 28 January 2021

Introduction

Why We're Speaking Volumes

In the summer of 2019, I was on the phone to Colin Grant, an author who's worked with Speaking Volumes for many years and also become a friend along the way. As usual, our conversation turned to the trials and tribulations of being people of colour working in the arts today. Colin told me a story about a recent experience he'd had.

A media outlet had asked him to write a piece on black writers' experiences in the UK publishing industry. So Colin decided to tackle some thorny topics — including the trend of mainstream publishers picking up new authors of colour to increase their diversity output, without offering them the editorial mentoring that *all* writers at that stage need to produce quality work. Inevitably, a book that isn't as good as it could be can lead to poorer reviews and sales — and, with it, the likelihood of that author finding it hard to secure another book deal. These are important issues to air, and they chime with many authors, not just black and brown ones; in fact, they can be encountered by anyone without knowledge or experience of the publishing world.

Yet when Colin submitted his well thought-out piece to the commissioning editor, he was told that it was *"not quite right for us"*. Whether this reaction was through fear of a backlash if they published anything negative about black authors – even though the piece was written by another black author – or something else, he was never told.

I was astounded. I know Colin to be an excellent writer, and that the piece would have only needed a light edit. But, in effect, it was deemed totally unpublishable. It showed me that, despite the fact that I've been working in publishing since 1994, so much still remains to be done to properly create an honest and genuinely level playing field in the creative industries, where we can *all* air our dirty – and clean – linen in public.

Fast forward a few weeks, and I'm talking to Sarah Sanders and Nick Chapman, my two colleagues at Speaking Volumes. We're discussing what to do to celebrate our tenth anniversary in 2020: a series of events maybe, themed around racial equality and social justice, the two issues at the heart of our organisation? Perhaps a book, glancing back and looking forward? We mull over ideas. By chance, just a short while later I meet Mitch Albert, editorial director at flipped eye publishing. Over lunch, we catch up on news and plans, and I casually mention the idea of a tenth-anniversary anthology. A few conversations later, the recollection of my conversation with Colin, a bit of thoughtful list-making of some of the authors we've worked with in our first decade and others with whom we'd like to work in the next … and *Not Quite Right for Us: Forty Authors Speak Volumes* was born. Along the way, the structure of the book also emerged, which focuses on humanity's universal preoccupations.

*

In 2010, Sarah and I decided to launch our own literature events organisation, having worked at PEN International together on two of its Free the Word! festivals. We both had part-time jobs, so we envisaged this new venture as a small operation, focusing on giving a platform to authors – from amongst the not-yet-published to stellar names – who were often missing from mainstream festivals or the pages of the literary supplements. Mainly, these were writers of colour; writers from lower socio-economic backgrounds; D/deaf and disabled writers and writers from abroad. We began with the odd commissioned job from other arts organisations, having settled on 'Speaking Volumes' as our name (an inspired suggestion from my friend, the novelist Pauline Melville).

On 8 November 2011, we signed a partnership agreement as a not-for-profit organisation, and were soon successful in our first application to Arts Council England — and, boy, wasn't it a big one, just shy of £122,000. We would work with the Southbank Centre to help deliver Poetry Parnassus, part of the Cultural Olympiad for the 2012 London Games. The Southbank would bring one poet from every Olympic country to London for events there, and we'd then organise a nationwide tour, including as much of the UK and as many poets as we could. Not such a small organisation anymore, then! Luckily, our other former PEN International colleague, Nick Chapman, readily agreed to come on board. A few months later, while the London Olympics played out on televisions around the world, we slumped on our respective sofas, having organised over thirty events with over fifty poets over a three-week period, taking them from Belfast to Cambridge, from Edinburgh to Devon. It was a great success, on time and on budget — but, most importantly, it showed us that we shouldn't limit the scale of our ambition. If we wanted to make real change, we needed to dream big.

Since then, our work has taken us up and down the UK countless times again, as well as to Belgium, Finland, Germany, Portugal, Spain and the USA. We've connected with authors in Australia and New Zealand, India and Pakistan, the Caribbean, Canada and across Europe. We've organised events for working-class Ranting protesting poets who've never been part of the genteel literature world; learned from D/deaf and disabled authors who refuse to be defined by patronising labels; curated events with Booker Prize-winning novelists who decline to play the establishment game; and showcased artists who've never published, and don't want to. We've put on literature events that don't look like literature events anywhere else, using film, music, images … wherever our imaginations take us.

Along the way, we've connected with so many people also working for change. Dr Maggi M. Morehouse, Burroughs Distinguished Professor at Coastal Carolina University in the USA, is known to us simply as 'Magpie at the Wheel', as she's not only sponsored many of our tours abroad, but even drove the minibus for us and our nine Black British authors when we visited California in 2015. She says: 'My reading life, my teaching life, my intellectual life, and yes, my dance party life, have all been enriched by my interaction and involvement with Speaking Volumes authors, poets, and artists.' (Yes, we do party hard…) Back here in the UK, independent producer Lucy Hannah notes that our 'commitment to underrepresented voices is total, and [Speaking Volumes'] professionalism and determination to reach new audiences is an inspiration.' Dominique Le Gendre, composer and artistic director at StrongBack Productions, says: 'My collaboration with Speaking Volumes constantly opens my eyes and affords me the personal and professional privilege of discovering poets of many voices, who can embody and translate the smallest human emotion and magnify it to reverberate for one and all.'

Whilst we're immensely proud of these very beautiful laurels, we're definitely not resting on them, as we know there's still a great deal of work to do, to show that the divisive *not quite right for us* can be transformed into *for one and all*, if you have the ambition and dream to do so.

Bring on the next decade.

Sharmilla Beezmohun

I childhood

'where in the curriculum does it say what/a child should do next?'

Alice, Lei Feng and Other Adventures in Childhood

Xiaolu Guo

I lived most of my life in rural China, then I left for the West. I was thirty when I first opened the pages of *Alice's Adventures in Wonderland*. Growing up in a small village, my early childhood was about scavenging for food in a harsh environment. If there was a wonderland in my dreams then, it was a *food* wonderland, with pork dumpling-filled ponds to swim in and beef-noodle beds to sleep on. We didn't have the luxury of children's literature or television to occupy our minds. In the 1970s and '80s, the legacy of the Cultural Revolution still permeated Chinese society. That bitter ideological wind had swept away all fairies and furry toys. Snow White never appeared in any theatre, nor the singing mermaids of Neverland; they were 'the opium of Western bourgeois society, instruments to narcotise children's minds'.

Now I realise that, from a Western point of view, I barely *had* a childhood. No one in 1960s and '70s China did; there was only propaganda for kids, forging an anti-Western and anti-feudal spirit. It got worse too. Teenage years came with the burden of school studies. Outside class, we had to absorb the lessons of the October Revolution by cramming Bulgakov's *White Guards* or stories about Yugoslav leader Tito's boyhood. Or we would learn facts about the French Revolution, how the heads of King Louis XVI and Marie-Antoinette had been chopped off. Apart from studying, there was always more studying. No time to play. So, no adolescence either.

Such were my early years. My mind – like those of my peers – was fattened by Communist dogma. And then, one morning, like cattle on the day of slaughter, we all awakened to a fevered capitalist hell, burning alive in it. '*Down with English–American*

Imperialism' suddenly appeared sarcastically as an opening line in a natively-produced rock 'n' roll song. One spring morning in 1994, I chanted those lines to myself while rushing to a newly opened computer store in Beijing. I queued with thousands of young people in order to buy a first-generation PC, only to be told they had all sold out. I sang the rock 'n' roll song again: '*Down with English–American Imperialism/ We are not afraid of paper tigers and materialism!*' Was this political rage or simply my own frustration against the computer industry? It felt to me that my generation was required to swallow one big contradiction; the state wanted us to talk the talk of socialism, but walk the walk of capitalism.

*

Decades later, centre-stage of the old capitalist world, England, I gave birth to my child in an east London hospital. Even before the baby had managed to open her eyes, we'd already received an ample supply of toys and music boxes and colouring books. So, I am, I realise, a childhood-less woman with a child in her arms. How will I ever be able to explain my history to this little girl? Now I have begun learning what a Western childhood might look like. Here in central London, we have free music classes for babies — not only in nurseries, but also in libraries and parks; we have play dates with kids dressed up as Batman; Tiny Tumble sessions almost every weekend. Every Monday there is baby yoga and every Wednesday, baby screening. When the days get darker and colder, children are promised Halloween parties, Christmas carol concerts and presents from Santa Claus; and in the summer, a beach holiday if the family has a good income … and so on. It's a paradise, or near-paradise, compared with kids in some other countries. Babyhood here is like a never-ending summer camp for young folk, with eternal sunny afternoons.

Two weeks after my child's birth, we were queuing at the town hall to register her as a British citizen. While waiting amongst many newborns and young parents, I opened a random page of *Alice's Adventures in Wonderland* and read:

'Curiouser and curiouser!' cried Alice. She was so much surprised, that for the moment she quite forgot how to speak good English; 'now I'm opening out like the largest telescope that ever was. Good-bye, feet!'

I began to wonder if there was any Chinese story vaguely resembling Lewis Carroll's. I went online and discovered a 1928 novel called *Alice's Adventures in China*, written by one of our most renowned writers, Shen Congwen. I immediately began reading the online version. Shen's Alice takes a trip to China with her white rabbit, in a political satire of a civil war-ravaged country. As I scanned the pages, I found the text heavy. The dialogue between the innocent Alice and Chinese peasants was totally rhetorical, choked with hardship and misery. Every character cried for social justice and the unavoidable revolution, including the rabbit. The book flopped, according to historians. I have to admit, though, that Alice's adventures in China are much more absurd than her journey down the rabbit hole — if absurdity is a necessary quality for children's literature.

But then, maybe the original Alice wasn't really for children in the first place, even if it's universally celebrated as children's literature. It was written for a repressed and square-minded adult society; especially *Through the Looking-Glass*, where the rule of the chess game is the narrative structure for the development of the plot. There is never a real character, only the patterns of a character according to the chess game. As I looked at the dialogue between the Red Queen and the young Alice, I could not help but wonder why there has been so little analysis about the political implications of Alice acting as a pawn under the command of the king and queen? She does seem to obey the rules of the game. But I suppose a non-Marxist society wouldn't offer such a critique of Alice's role. The absence of that kind of analysis, perhaps, is logical: Britain still hasn't had a proper revolution; the working class still doesn't play as much chess as the rich do. Here another thought popped into my mind. Maybe people in Victorian society didn't have a 'childhood' either, as in my 1970s China ... I began thinking of Dickens's *Oliver Twist*, with its inhuman workhouses, hunger, abuse and children slaving six days a week. Was that a world without childhood — or was childhood reserved for the elite? If you look at those dollhouses in the V&A Museum of Childhood in London, you realise all those toys were highly prized and specially made for wealthy families.

Well, perhaps childhood is indeed a lifestyle belonging to the elite in the West. On the other hand, my natural fascination with authors rather than their books urges me to ask: did Charles Dodgson, the man who wrote under the name of 'Lewis Carroll', write Alice to recover a childhood he'd never had, or was his infatuation with the real young Alice the result of the 'gaze' and longing?

I wonder: is there a 'natural' childhood for children to just be? If so, what happened in my Communist China or in their Victorian Britain? Why were these versions of childhood so different? Is the so-called 'natural' childhood smothered by cruel social forces? Or does the specific culture of childhood create childhood as we know it? It seems to me that childhood is a cultural invention, as much as 'adolescence' is. In some aboriginal cultures the world over, boys of a certain age undertake a 'rite of passage' to become warriors. That can mean going off into the bush to connect with their totems, hunting certain kinds of animals, following designated songlines: enforced separation, expulsion from the tribe and, finally, a return under a different identity. The metamorphosis from child to man is carried out through living practice and culturally invested meanings. In any case, what we now call 'adolescence' is a twentieth-century invention, shaped and theorised during the postwar period in the United States and Europe. From the 1950s onwards, psychologists such as Erik Erikson, Anna Freud and Glen Elder formulated their theories about adolescence. The rebellious teenager had to undergo radical physical change and confusion, battling emotions they could not understand, and when this internal turmoil met the realities of complex postwar society, the internal conflict only intensified. James Dean's roles in *Rebel Without a Cause* and *East of Eden* are cultural archetypes, manifesting that transition period towards adulthood.

It seems self-evident that childhood is manufactured, both in the East and the West. Childhood in the latter today is like a children's television channel; despite the fun and innocence, it is still nevertheless embedded in the systematic production of a consumer society. When I see and feel this commercial force permeating every corner of children's lives here, I ask: is it actually *better* to be without a so-called childhood? When I voiced this thought to an English friend, she scoffed at such an absurd notion. Okay. But I felt stifled by my secret status; being an adult without childhood.

Thinking back, one of the Chinese children's idols I grew up with was a young solider named Lei Feng of the People's Liberation Army. He died when he was twenty-one. Always wearing an army uniform and carrying a rifle, for the last fifty years he has beamed forth from propaganda posters, surrounded by slogans such as: *Follow Lei Feng's example: love the Party, love Socialism, love the People.* From our earliest school days, we learned how selfless Lei Feng had been, how he'd dedicated every single minute of his life to the greater good. Well, that was our primary education: to learn to be entirely selfless, without vanity and not to be daydreamers. In the 1960s, *Lei Feng's Diary* was first presented to the public by Lin Biao, then Vice Chairman of the Chinese Communist Party, in the 'Learn from Lei Feng' campaigns. The diary was full of accounts of Lei's admiration for Mao Zedong, his self-sacrificing deeds and his desire to foment revolutionary spirit. The campaign lasted till the mid 1990s.

But time's arrow has not brought us a new living Lei Feng in any form. The eternal fire of Lei Feng's Communist spirit has cooled somewhat in early twenty-first-century China. Indeed, it has become digital. In 2006, a Chinese organisation released a video game titled *Learn from Lei Feng Online*, in which the player has to perform good deeds, fight spies and amass objects from Mao Zedong's collection. If the player wins, their character gets to meet Mao. It looks like a postmodern joke, but not in China's self-transforming new spirit.

*

Back in east London, at our local town hall, we waited in the queue for our child's birth registration and finally witnessed the blue stamp landing loudly on a freshly produced document. We thanked the man behind the counter and walked out of the registration office with satisfaction. As we exited, we passed a line of babies in prams, pushed by their mixed-race parents. These babies, I guessed – perhaps half-Nigerian/half-English, or half-Iranian/half-French – will receive bilingual or trilingual educations. And in lots of cases, English will be the third language in their homes. These little persons will be reading *Alice's Adventures in Wonderland* with a Latin American inflection, or *Peter Pan* with a Russian accent, or Hans Christian Andersen's fables with a Muslim background. And perhaps Alice will morph into some new kind of narrative in childhood's future: Alice wearing a Palestinian keffiyeh; Alice, with her dark skin, running in the Sahara desert; Alice donning her abaya every morning...

Days flew by. We celebrated my little girl's first birthday. Under her glittering gaze, I blew out a solitary candle for her. I saw something I could barely imagine, a kind of wonderland in her dark brown eyes. I thought it might be possible that, away from my ideological China and away from Victorian Britain, this little person could have a childhood without the stamp of an imposed identity. The world out there might be manufacturing illusions of instant happiness with alluring toys and plastic choices. Still, she and I could make our childhood together, along with the help of a shape-changing rabbit.

The Wrong Clothing

John Hegley

My brother's suit's too big for me.
It smells of cigarette smoke so,
but I decide to step inside
and risk my first school disco.
You'll be there, and I will dare to share with you
my disco fever.

On my arrival, Thompson's in a T-shirt
and looking round, I clearly see
oversize formality is not the way to be tonight.
There's not another brother's suit in sight.

I can't recall exactly just how awkward
is my asking you to dance.
I remember how reluctantly you join me on the dance floor.
It's more of a scuffle than a dance.
So, I go and blow my disco chance.

Then there is the raffle,
the announcement of the winner
of the two-bob lucky voucher to spend at the tuck-shop counter.
I call out, 'HEY, that winning number's mine!'
There isn't any cheering when I do.
I fear I may hear Thompson going 'Boo.'

I wanted to assign you a swig of my pop
and the option of a winning Crunchie bar.

At least I have the sense to see
eyes that are not there for me,
that do not drink complicity,
my brother's suit's too big for me
and upstairs on the bus, on my way home
I eat up all those sweeties feeling bitter to the bone.
I consume those Crunchies on my own.

Off the bus, when I get back,
before the suit is on the rack,
my little sister wants to know
'How did it go
down the disco?'
I slacken in an armchair
I give it a few moments and I say
'You see this raffle ticket?'
She sees the raffle ticket and I say,
'You're looking at a winner, by the way.'

Hey! Coffee!

Catherine Johnson

I have a charmed life. I was born not long after the mid-point of the twentieth century, when children went everywhere on their own. I spent long days on the covered reservoir or playing over the allotments or in the gardens of derelict houses. In places where the grass was so long you could make dens and no one would know you were there.

My parents were warned not to have children. We would be, at the very least, mad. It was unfair; we'd be not one thing or the other, no one would want us, not white people nor black people. We'd be confused.

But, Mum said, isn't everyone?

My mum loved showing me off. She dressed me in white and yellow. She cut my hair short so she didn't have to brush it. And both my parents always made me feel I was more than good enough; at home, the world was at my feet.

And I'm definitely a glass-half-full sort of woman. The universe has been kind. I've been blessed – so far – with health, symmetrical features and a dollop of good luck. I may no longer be a marriageable woman, but I am happy in my skin. I'm light-skinned brown. The sort of brown that screams citizen of everywhere — or nowhere. A high-yellow woman with good hair. The sort of curls that elderly women who like perms admire. An acceptable shade of tan. People – white people – stop me in the street, lean over in the train (or they did in the before times) and tell me what a lovely colour I am — *just the shade they'd like to be.*

Once, the year before last, in the summer, I was driving, waiting at a T-junction, arm on the open window, when two women staggered off a bus, vodka bottles in hand. They lurched towards me in a drunken run. I desperately wished for a gap in the traffic, the chance to pull away. None came.

The first woman to reach me leaned down, her arm on my arm, grinning, like she had discovered cold fusion or perpetual motion. 'That colour! See?' she looked from me to our arms, brown skin next to white, to her mate hurrying to catch up. 'That's the colour I want!'

I did not flinch. I knew not to. I kept the smile sort of on my face and drove away as soon as I could. I felt part funny, part odd; part – in that moment when I clocked the two of them drunk and closing in – scared.

And that sums it up really; every reaction, every interaction. I think it's about keeping your face straight, making sure your cast-iron heart is mostly impervious and hoping that glass-half-full doesn't get smashed in your face.

Of course, I am so much more of what people want than my parents were. No one has refused me a flat or a home. No one told me not to marry whoever I wanted or would deny me access to contraception. I have one of those faces that could be anything. I could be anyone. Whatever it is you project: Israeli, Moroccan, Tahitian, Javanese. Everything … or nothing.

And now at my age, in these times, it's easier, I present as a nice, middle-class, grey-haired divorcee; likes ponies, swimming, knitting, cinema, good food and wine (sometimes). I know who I am now and have taken to calling myself English – both parents would be very upset at this – but surely that's what I am. Not a Londoner anymore. I live in Hastings; I am thoroughly, entirely, to the tips of my fingers, one of the Angle folk. A sister through time to Beachy Head Woman across the bay in Eastbourne. Here to stay. Even if I'm not quite what anyone wants.

But then, this morning at the council pool, it happened again. I had spoken to this man before – a fellow swimmer – about not putting on a 1970s *It Ain't Half Hot, Mum* Indian accent when he speaks to me, but clearly he enjoys it, wants a reaction perhaps. My face is blank, but inside it's 1969 all over again.

I must be seven or eight. I'm on the beach at Pensarn, north Wales, my mum and her sister are somewhere down the beach talking, and talking fast, in Welsh and English, and eating Lyons Jersey slices: ersatz cream, flaky pastry, with a faint, gritty dusting of sand.

Out on the mauve sea, big boats on the horizon plough up and down between Liverpool and everywhere else.

I am up away from the sea, away from Mum, up where the road runs into the pebbly, sandy, nothingy beach from town. To where the donkeys are.

There is a donkey man – flat-capped, sort of screw-faced from lack of teeth and a lifetime of squinting – and a donkey boy, browned by the sun and not genetics, wearing, I think, a kind of ink-blue Bri-Nylon turtleneck top, whatever the weather.

I am rapt. It is love, I think. Those big eyes, the long ears, the velvety, velvety, noses. The hooves, the fur, the smell. Even the saddles and bridles. Ancient leather, brow bands with their names painted on with old enamel paint in seaside-y primary colours: Flash, Smokey, Rosie.

I am there all the time. Every time. Every visit. How much is a ride? Sixpence, I think, but I could be wrong. When the sixpences are done, I hang around. I hang around so much that sometimes, if there are a lot of punters, I get to lead the little ones across the top of the beach. And it makes me I feel, I think, the way a king might.

The donkey man calls me 'Coffee.' He shouts it down the beach: 'Hey! Coffee!'

It's not my name, but I don't correct him.

I am not stupid.

I am not rocking this four-legged boat.

Lessons in Assholery

Jay Bernard

History

What causes me to type your name?
It's late and I am three beers in when you appear,

a genie of the search terms: you + London,
your last name + dead, you + our old school.

Now I know of time as tin-opener,
cuts in circles, leaves a hinge.

The grey waters that we pour away.
Had someone thought to teach a class on love

I might
know you.

Geography

We sometimes walked the back way home
past my house so I could shake you off.

Writing now, I want to make this the story
of two working-class kids but there are degrees

to work and class, and I am pissed off with,
or ashamed by, the two-up two-down fantasy,

when the truth is that after Pokémon
I'd kick you out – because if my mother met you –

like the time when we got to your door
and your mother dragged you in by the neck –

where in the curriculum does it say what
a child should do next?

Drama

Standing up in the dining hall
and offering your meal
to the poorest student
in your class.

Music

Between Googles I watch compilation videos of top ten worst
auditions for *X-Factor*. I don't find it funny, just compelling,
like folk art. Almost all of them are mentally ill in one way or
another and almost all of them confess this right away – in their
teeth, their shitty style, their choice of song – and most of them
are poor. The interesting bit is when they're done and Simon
asks, 'What was that?' and they say they might not be the best
singer now, but they've got potential. I don't think many of
them are looking for fame, really, but want to be taken on. Fed,
trained, blow-dried like a Pomeranian. But they've bit their
nails to porridge, their feet sweat through their shoes. And
Simon says, you can't sing, just as I once told a girl in my class
that she would amount to nothing, and in the heat that ensues,
their argument is less *whether* they can reach the crescendo of
'I Will Always Love You', but that if someone treated them
nicely, they could.

PSHE

I was sent an email once,
by someone explaining that they would not help me

because I was flaky, inconsistent, rude,
non-collegiate, unworthy of anything I had.

He, too, was from Clarendon, my old ancestral land
and for a second I feared the Old Testament God

who still reigns there, had reversed my salvation:

'I was extremely surprised – amazed and even dumbfounded,
to be very honest – against my own will, I found myself wondering
how you could be working there, and more astonishingly,
keeping the position. But so far you seem to be
doing well there, so my warmest congratulations!!'

The world tells you everything that will happen.
I knew then what I know now.

The heart has a tendency to plump
in advance of the laceration.

Dance

Walking home through Spitalfields
a man shakes his bucket for mental health.
I have no cash so I refuse.

He doesn't care about the change,
he seems to know what I have done.

You people are unbearable,
you know that? You people around here
are unbearable.

The Freshie Rocker

afshan d'souza-lodhi

This year is the second time in my life that I'm sporting an undercut, a type of hairstyle that features shaving a large portion of your head. Because the shaved part of the head is usually the under-layer near the nape of the neck or to one side, it's pretty easy to hide with long hair. And that's exactly what I've done, hidden it: from my mum, from the nosy aunties who stalk my Instagram and the uncles who hang about the meat shop. It's really silly to think that I meticulously shaved (or, rather, strong-armed my friend into meticulously shaving) the underside of my head, only for me to spend most of the time with my hair down, hiding the shaved part. I just know that in Manchester, even in 2020, we desis haven't reached a point when we can sport a shaved (or even partially shaved) hairstyle.

I wasn't always like this, a wannabe rocker. There was a moment when I could have been identified as an uncool 'freshie'.

I was thirteen when my dad gave me an MP3 player. He told me it was like an iPod, but better. This one had speakers attached to it, so when you took the headphones out you could blast your music. Who needed headphone splitters?

Now, here I could go into detail about a certain incident but, honestly, it still makes me nauseous. All I'll say is that it involved my high-school crush, a public bus, some cringe Bollywood music and the not-an-iPod-MP3 player. That was the last time I used it — and it was also the first time I used Limewire to download the most recent edition of *Now That's What I Call Music*. Never again would I be caught listening to high-pitched tones over tabla beats in public. I wasn't old enough or politically aware enough to understand the term 'assimilation' but, in hindsight, that's what it was. I did not want to be singled out for being different; I was already one of only two hijabis in my school, and the other one was much cooler than me.

I remember the first time I listened to rock music. My friend Charlotte burnt me a mixtape on some CDs titled *Songs to get Angry to*, featuring rock and some heavy metal. This is how I was introduced to Nirvana, Linkin Park, Red Jumpsuit Apparatus, Blink 182, Papa Roach and Blue October. From there it was a short jump to Five Finger Death Punch and Rammstein. This music made me angry, made me want to scream, but in a cathartic way. I felt safe and protected while listening to it.

Eventually my ringtones would be replaced with heavy guitar strumming, and I'd wake up to 'I chose death before dishonour' and start my day. I used to wonder if people could hear the screaming through my headphones. Luckily for me, my hijab style back then consisted of wrapping thick material round and round my head pretty tightly, creating a soundproofing effect.

I don't think I ever thought too deeply about the lyrics; I just really liked how I could zone out to the noise. This is in complete contrast to the Bollywood music I had grown up listening to.

Pretty soon my wardrobe began to change too: leather jackets, NEW ROCKS on my feet. I even invested in some chains for my hijab. I was determined to look the part and fit in.

The first concert I went to was Rammstein.[1] I got all kitted out in a faux-leather skirt, some ripped tights and a choker. I turned up with my friend at the O2, but it was only when we were walking up the stairs to our seats that I realised everyone around me was white. The whole venue was full of industrial-metal fans. I struggled to find one person of colour.

A few months later, I went to see Marilyn Manson and exactly the same thing happened; a full arena and not one person of colour in sight. As we left that concert, someone spilled a glass of beer on me. It was most probably an accident, but that small act suddenly made the space unsafe. I didn't go to a mosh pit again after that. Something didn't feel right.

I started questioning the politics and race of the musicians. Suddenly I became hyper-aware of the alt-right and neo-Nazis, and their chosen anthems — all metal. My love for the music eventually died down, yet the aesthetic stayed.

I tried hard to find rock and punk bands that had people of colour in them, particularly desis. But it seemed like punk wasn't something desis did. And then I came across The Kominas. The Kominas did for me what those first CDs from Charlotte had done. They provided me with a safe space to be desi *and* Muslim *and* punk, to be able to swear and scream and headbang. The Kominas allowed me back into the punk and rock spheres without feeling like I was sympathising with the alt-right. The only problem was that they were based in the United States. I couldn't find a community here in Manchester.

I moved back in with my parents, and had to tone down my rock-chick look massively. None of my desi friends were into it; they didn't really get why I wanted to shave my head or understand the appeal of a scaffold piercing. My ripped denim jackets were replaced with kurtas; my leather chains and cuffs with gold bangles. In the mainstream, we started seeing desi influencers and models. Sari-inspired clothing and bindis made their way through hipster clubs and festivals and into fashion weeks. I didn't have time to mourn the loss of the leather. I had a new obsession.

My mother was happier seeing me in 'culturally appropriate' clothing. I quickly got bored of the femme look and tried to switch it up, wearing short kurtas with jeans and baggy shalwars with normal T-shirts. It didn't go down too well. For some reason, when white girls did it, it was fashion, but when I did it, it looked like I'd forgotten half the outfit at home. I didn't understand how yoga pants and casually worn bindis had finally become a fashion statement for others, but gave me 'high school freshie' flashbacks when I wore them. I yearned for the times when I could just wear leather skirts and chokers and instantly feel part of a community.

I also missed listening to metal. I fell in and out of love with people who introduced me to other genres of music, but I could never recreate the feeling I got when I listened to metal. I had a brief moment of listening to bhangra and then to Afrobeat, but found that I was always looking for heavy beats and something to zone out to.

I started going to Muslim matchmaking events but, ultimately, had to make a choice. I could either embrace my half-punk, half-desi self and try and explain all of that in the space of two minutes, or I could drop one of them. It was always easier to drop one. I knew the 'cultured' and desi version of myself would be more accepted in those spaces, so I put the leather jacket back in the closet. The matchmaking never amounted to anything; the events were great for anecdotes to tell at parties, but nothing else. Even with my 'cultured, desi' self, I was still not right for those events or those spaces. I just didn't fit in. It's a shame it took me a while to work that out.

A few months ago, I found a suitcase containing my old leather skirts, corsets and ripped tights. I tried on my leather jacket and found that it didn't fit. I'd outgrown it. Perhaps because of the lockdown, or perhaps it was knowing that the aunties will always side-eye me, I ordered a new jacket and a pair of chunky Doc Martens, and called a friend to shave my head.

As a teen I used to dream of starting my own desi punk band. Maybe I'll call it The Real Freshies.[2] Maybe I'll bump into a few desis who love headbanging and wearing baggy shalwars as much as I do, and we'll start a band together. In the meantime, I'll keep listening to The Kominas on repeat and hiding my undercut from my mum.

Notes

[1] OK, so this is a semi-lie I tell people. It was actually Justin Bieber (three days earlier!) but, in my defence, I was accompanying my sister and so it doesn't count.

[2] The Freshies were an actual punk band in Manchester in the 1970s.

II family

'And you, Nana, are you a cousin or who?'

Mad, Bad and Dangerous to Know

Byron Vincent

It's 26 February, 1975. I really don't want to be born; I have to be induced. Can you blame me? Some sleep-deprived medic grabs my quaggy skull, yanks me into the blinding light, dangles me upside down like a string of uncooked sausages and slaps me until I cry.

Welcome to the world, cheeky-chimp, it's all downhill from here.

The name on my birth certificate is 'Byron Vincent Baden Nuttall'. The 'Byron' is after Lord Byron, a man as famous for shagging his sister as he is for his poetry. The 'Vincent' is after Vincent Van Gogh, not exactly an exemplar of reason and coherency. I mean, I'm not saying they weren't geniuses. Let's just hope that if I'm going to share anything at all with my namesakes, it's their creative talents and not their proclivities for incest and self-harm. I probably am a genius; at least that's what Mum reckons. According to her, at ten months old my conversational fluency is so advanced that it freaks out strangers. Nan, a hardy sparrow of a woman with architectural hair and a penchant for maroon velour leisure suits, agrees. *He's an old soul*, she says through a fog of hairspray, perfume and menthol cigarette smoke.

I'm a very affectionate baby — clingy, some might argue. I cry. *A lot.* I'll be a toddler before my mum can go anywhere without me clamped to her like a limpet. Abandon me for a second and I wail like a slapped banshee. I love my mum to pieces; we develop an incredibly close bond. *Mummy's boy*, that's what my sister will call me.

Fortunately, I'm born with *the gift*. A psychic sensitivity. That's what Nan reckons, and she's half gypsy. Cynics can scoff all they like, but this isn't just wild conjecture. Nan, a semi-professional tarot reader and astrologer, can decipher your fate from a few old tea leaves. She keeps a crystal ball perched on a swatch of purple silk as the centrepiece to her ever-increasing legion of ceramic clowns. She knows a thing or two about spiritual exceptionalism — and she isn't the only one. Mum is a practising Wiccan, often found in full robes performing occult rituals under a full moon on the bit of grass outside our council flat. She has an extensive New Age library containing *Out on a Limb* by Shirley MacLaine and the complete works of David Icke. There's further evidence too. New-born babies' eyesight is supposed to be terrible. Not mine. Within minutes of being born, my eyes follow the nurses around the room like a creepy painting. The midwife summons other staff members and they come in droves to marvel. *Look at this child, how weird*. Everyone agrees that I'm special. The eye thing is definitely a sign.

By the time I turn three, my exceptionalism is even more pronounced. Whilst most toddlers are struggling to repeat their own names and shoving Lego up their nostrils, I appear to be developing a more nuanced understanding of the world. I can read all Mum's flashcards *and* I know what the word *ambidextrous* means.

'Ask him what "ambidextrous" means,' Mum boasts to anyone who will listen. I dutifully respond by writing my name with both hands. I write it backwards, but still.

As my perceived genius grows, so does my sensitivity. I'm anxious about pretty much everything. Broken biscuits, the dark, even the sound of my own heartbeat. You name it, I have a burgeoning phobia about it. Every night I have horrific nightmares: sometimes abstract hellscapes populated by nothing but giant, ominous cups of milky tea (scarier than it sounds); other times, more literal. A recurrent theme is hearing Nazi jackboots marching up the stairs to take me away.

One day Mum overhears me singing the jaunty World War One classic from the trenches, 'Daisy Bell', and she freaks out. I know all the words. How could this be? The ensuing conversation goes as follows:

Mum: *Where did you learn that song?*
Me: *I know it from when I was here before.*

Mum: *What do you mean 'here before'?*

Me (frustrated): *When I was Tom, in the war.*

Mum: *And what happened to Tom?*

At this point, my head cranes like an eerie ventriloquist's dummy. I stare her directly in the eye and say: *I died in the mud.*

I'm a creepy little shit, but I mean well.

Nan posits that I'm more than likely the reincarnated soul of a deeply traumatised soldier, which is probably why I have the gift. This is why I'm … different. I'm obviously just a little too closely aligned to the spirit world. Mum concurs.

By four I've developed the unshakeable suspicion that I don't belong in this world. I've obviously been dropped off here by mistake. The mothership is going to come and collect me any day now, you'll see.

I'm too delicately tuned for this place. The shapes are jarring. The necklines itch. The noises are shrill and unsettling. My hands feel weird. *Do my hands look weird to you? They look weird to me.* I'll often stare at them or focus on a spot on the busy Seventies wallpaper until I enter a dissociative state.

Me: *Is any of this real? What is reality?*

Mum: *Eat your chips.*

I'm full of love, but frightened, confused and appalled by half the things people do. I just don't understand why they are so mean to one another; it's totally illogical. What purpose does it serve? Just the thought of all the cruelty in the world gives me this horrible feeling in my chest that hardly ever subsides. It keeps me awake. It will keep me awake for decades to come. And don't you dare call me naïve either; I'm a child sceptic. I've already figured out that there's no Santa. *Listen, the reindeer are coming,* they'd say on Christmas Eve. It's clearly just Dad ringing a bell from behind the sofa; I can't work out if the grown-ups are idiots or if they just think that we are.

Me: *If the universe is infinite, how do we know there isn't a meteor a hundred times the size of our sun hurtling towards us right now?*

Mum: *If you don't go to bed, Santa won't come.*

The problem is that not everyone is as encouraging about my paranormal talents as Mum and Nan. One day I make an announcement to some of the estate kids. I'm like, *I have supernatural powers. I can summon your dead granddad. We can still be pals, so don't even worry about it.*

Unfortunately, instead of the awe and adulation I'd hoped to inspire, they chase me home and corner me in my doorway. I hammer desperately on the frosted glass, but I know full well that Mum is out at one of her cleaning jobs. No one is coming to help. I threaten to release an army of the dead on them as they spit and jeer. But they're unfazed. Rocks the size of my fist crack off my head. I can feel the lumps forming. Deep down I understand that when it comes to being rescued, ghosts and parents are consistently unreliable.

It's 1980. I'm five years old. I have little skinny legs with knock-knees that look like knots in pipe cleaners, a wonky bowl cut courtesy of Mum and an angelic little freckled face that apparently looks quite feminine, because I get mistaken for a girl a lot. My sister's hand-me-downs don't help. People say I'm unusually affectionate for a boy. I take it as a compliment. I like hugs. They help quiet this constant unease in me, this underlying hum of threat, the knowing in my middle that things are not as they should be.

Beams of light strobe across my face as I run through the large oak trees around the back of my dad's workshop. I reckon these trees are big enough to live in. I've decided that when I grow up, I'm going to live in a tree. I'm watching a sparrow flitting about when a cat leaps out of nowhere, clamping the terrified bird in its jaws. For a moment, I am that bird. I feel its terror, its heart racing in my chest. It seems so brutal. Why are things like this? Not by design, surely. I guess that makes me an atheist. 'Supernaturally gifted atheist' is one of the many paradoxical roles I'll take on in my young life, but for now I'm so shocked at this feline violence that I burst into tears and run into the workshop where Mum and Dad are chatting to three blokes. Seventies blokes. All mutton-chops, double denim and Hai Karate aftershave. They're utterly baffled as to why I'm so upset. *He's a very sensitive boy*, Mum offers in a tone that's apologetic, but also proud; after all, I *do* have *the gift*.

She's right about me being unusually sensitive. Forty years later, while making a documentary for the BBC, I'll find out I have the 'orchid gene', an anomalous genetic variant that apparently predisposes one to hypersensitivity. But there's no room for that kind of hysterical quackery here. In 1980, any man with flowers in his DNA is no man at all. Men drive FORD Capris, shag birds and throw half-bricks at each other at football matches. Age five, I'm more your hiding-in-cupboards-with-a-selection-of-illustrated-reference-books sort of guy.

Their judgment is written all over their aggressively hirsute faces. *He's a soft lad* — the worst of all the lads. It feels frustratingly reductive. Is that all we are to each other? A set menu of traits for people we barely know to smash together to form the intractable narrative of our characters?

Too sensitive. Too soft. Aren't I more than that? I'll hear those words or less polite synonyms often over the ensuing years, usually when I'm expected to fight, but don't want to. The problem is that people who want to fight tend not to give a shit whether or not *you* do. Violence happens regardless, and the kicks and punches don't just injure, they sculpt. Every split lip and bloody nose alters us. Every humiliation is a step change in a metamorphosis. We begin to calcify, to lose feeling in the parts of ourselves where feeling counts. Dormant parts begin to burn. Feelings become uncontrollable and explosive. Eventually, we're changed into something hard, combustible, disconnected.

Later that year Dad leaves, taking the reindeer bells with him. He's the first to go. I'll say goodbye to them all before adolescence is done.

It's 1994. I'm handcuffed to a hospital bed. I'm nineteen years old. They've left a WPC in the room with me. Dunno why; I'm in no state to abscond. I guess she's here to subdue me if I do try to kick off. She's giving me that look, like she'd love to empty a can of pepper spray in my face. Like I'm scum.

It's the same look you get from shop detectives or from those smug pricks at the Department of Social Security when you ask for a crisis loan. A couple of hours earlier, I'd been arrested by an armed SWAT team for possession of a firearm. Those boys don't mess about. They did a proper job on me. Slammed me into the concrete and spread me out crucifixion-style. One of them dropped his full body weight on me, knee to face. Fourteen stone, driving my cheekbone into the paving slab. The river of alcohol and barbiturates coursing through my bloodstream meant I'd felt very little at the time. The throb is just now beginning to creep through my Temazepam fug, reverberating around my skull, trailing *the fear* with it like a dragged corpse. I have a gunshot wound through the palm of my hand from an incident a couple of weeks back. There's no missing it, swaddled in grubby bandages. My hand had swollen like a tennis ball after the surgery, so one of these bastards decides to stomp on it. Brings the heel of his big, black tactical boot down on it until it bursts. I'm nothing if not a cheerleader for the anaesthesia of benzodiazepines, but even in my senseless state, that hurt like a motherfucker. That's why I'm here and not in the cells. My mangled hand was pissing claret all over the back seat of their shiny FORD Focus, so they have to stitch me back up before they can process me.

I'm not saying I didn't deserve it. What was I thinking? This is bad. I guess I'm lucky I didn't get shot. So many close calls. I was resuscitated from overdoses more times than I can remember over the last year. You think they'd get the message. I shouldn't fucking be here. I try not to think about it. Bury it. My hands are shaking; I try to tell myself it's just opiate withdrawal, I've been smashing fistfuls of benzos every day for god knows how long; but it's not just that. I'm not allowed to say it, not even to myself, but truth is: I'm frightened.

Take away the drugs and all that's left is fear. My pad mate has been shagging a local sex worker called Little Shel. She comes and crawls into my bed whenever he does her head in and she's too mashed to wobble home. She told me that not only do I scream in my sleep, I punch and kick too. I said I was sorry, and she just laughed and stroked my hair. That felt really nice.

It's weird trynna make breakie knowing that there are people out there who want you dead. They said that if they ever caught up with us they'd nail us to trees and disembowel us whilst we were still alive. They'd do it too. Images glitch into my thoughts. I try not to focus on them. A knife to my face. Stinging pain. Blood. Waves of fear. Nausea. Don't let them get a foothold. Don't show this copper you're scared. Don't give her the satisfaction.

We never know what's gonna traumatise us. When I was being tortured it wasn't the hot-sticky pain of the Stanley knife slicing down my back that I couldn't handle, it was the fact that I was shirtless. My scrawny limbs and emaciated ribs seemed so pathetic and ineffectual compared to these bigger, older men. Like a desperate bird in the jaws of a feral cat. Let them come and try that shit again, I'll fucking kill them.

Would you? Then why are you hiding?

SHUT THE FUCK UP! I wish I could shut myself up. I don't even know who I am anymore. That copper thinks she knows who I am. She thinks I'm one hundred per cent undiluted trouble. A set menu from a greasy spoon with a zero hygiene rating and a snide cook who gobs in the gravy. The intractable narrative is written across her face in such bold capitalised text that I can read it over here in the cheap seats.

YOU'RE A WRONG 'UN AND YOU NEED LOCKING UP.

Maybe she's right. Whenever I leave the house I imagine fighting every bloke unfortunate enough to stumble into my orbit. Play out violent scenarios like psychotic video games. Could I take that big guy? Maybe if I grabbed that pool cue or wrapped that bottle around his head. Funny, but the last thing I want to do is hurt anyone. Not that I could ever admit to that. So I spend every waking minute preparing for the worst. I always sit with my back to a wall so I can see threats coming. I always know it's gonna kick off way before it does; it's like I'm psychic. I make sure everyone knows I'm not to be fucked with. Stare down strangers in the street. Give 'em that *get the fuck out of my way* look. Men twice my size averting their gaze. If someone who looks a bit handy starts throwing shade my way, then fuck it, I might as well start on 'em. I mean, I'll get my head kicked in, but at least it'll be on my terms. If I play it like I don't give a fuck, that news'll travel. Then maybe the next dickhead'll think twice.

I thought I'd grow up to be a pacifist. Ha! The only time I'm not thinking about violence is when I'm too fucked to care. How long has this writhing ball of anxiety been eating me from the inside out? When was the last time I woke up without wondering if today would be my last? Hoping it would be. That's why I try to stay zombified for the hours that I'm conscious. But it's gotta be around three AM now. My opioid superpowers are wearing off. Feeling is returning, and that's the absolute worst, because there's nothing inside me that feels good. I wish I was dead. I wish someone would get it over with and kill me.

The copper leans forward and I can just tell she's about to have another dig. Fucking prick.

WPC: *I've spoken to the doctor. We have your files. You've really been through the wars, haven't you?*

Her voice is soft, caring.

I remember being off school with the measles. I'm six, swaddled in my Superman duvet. Mum's sat on my bed stroking my hair. She *did* love me.

I feel my eyes watering. I plead with myself: *Don't you fucking dare.*

Only for a Short While

Cheryl Martin

Oh, only for so short a while you
have loaned us to each other,
because we take form in your act of drawing us,
and we take life in your painting us,
and we breathe in your singing us.

But only for so short a while
have you loaned us to each other.
Because even a drawing cut in obsidian fades,
and the green feathers, the crown feathers,
of the Quetzal bird lose their colour,
and even the sounds of the waterfall
die out in the dry season.

So, we too, because only for a short while
have you loaned us to each other.
– Aztec prayer*

Only for a short while
We are loaned to each other
We never see each other as we are
We never know each other as we are
We can only see reflections of ourselves
In each other's eyes
We can only hear echoes
Of our own voices inside our heads
Never the voice another hears
Never the face another sees
Never the life another lives

We never show each other
Our lives in full
For fear
We're afraid our own sadness
Will engulf you,
And we love you
So want to spare you that

We never tell each other
Of the father nearly tarred and feathered
Of the universities our uncles and aunts couldn't enter
Of the brother who was lynched
Of the illegitimate children hidden in plain sight
Of the abandonments and betrayals that gave birth to them
Of growing up black hillbillies with loads of books
Smart, smart, viper-tongued and beautiful
Minds so sharp outsiders can only be cut to pieces
That's what outsiders are for
You passed it all down to us
The infallible eye for the expensive
The unquenchable ambition, the expansive
Intellects – smart, smart, viper-tongues and beautiful –
Marching through Cambridge and Princeton and Yale
We are the future our great-grandparents couldn't even dream
        of
Not the indigenous, not the immigrant, not coloniser nor the
        colonised
Not the Native American slavers nor the East Coast slaves
We are the future they never knew could happen
We are the distillation of all their longing
The brilliant generation
Crystallised perfection
Lawyers and chemists and poets and artists and playwrights
A single civil servant, a nod to the uncles and aunts
Teachers and accountants
We are what they wished for

And I love them, mother, grandmother, uncles, aunts
So I never tell them
All the pretty prizes, all the successes
The degrees, the commissions, the scholarships, the
        productions,
The films, the books, the every-fucking-thing
Glittering mirages from someone else's life
Unreal
I know how that would make them feel
So I never say it

Because we are only loaned to each other
For such a short while.
So why not make them smile?
I would not live this life again.
That's what I can never tell them.

*Aztec prayer quoted in Praying Our Goodbyes: The Spirituality
of Change by Joyce Rupp, 1988.

Prodigal

Maame Blue

Flying to him meant taking herself somewhere she didn't belong. It was never a journey or a discovery; it was just being somewhere, and then being somewhere else. Nana thought about this as she watched the chunk of money she'd been saving for a new laptop disappear from her account. BRITISH AIRWAYS thanked her with a confirmation email. She mused over things as she sat in Terminal 5 at Heathrow Airport, its vastness suggesting numerous ways to escape if you only had the means. Naturally she treated herself to a McDONALD's breakfast, the Sausage and Egg McMuffin filling her up for the ten minutes she needed to review her text messages.

She considered the trip to him, to Paa Kwesi, as a movement that churned in her stomach along with her weightless breakfast. Everything about him felt indefinite and nebulous. She did not know which way to move within her feelings for him, so she didn't. She shut them off as she found her window seat in Premium Economy, slightly more legroom and inches-more seat space so that her thighs were not mashed up against the sides like they had been the last time she'd taken a flight. There was only excitement then, after she'd snapped up a budget-airline deal to visit a friend in Paris. That trip had been years ago — or maybe it was only weeks? It was hard to be sure about time these days. But she could ponder over Paa Kwesi endlessly, as if he was stuck in one timeframe, a frozen image of reproach. Even after all the years that they hadn't spoken.

She had been dreading the trip, as she always did; the rise of the wheels, the lift-off from the runway, passengers encased in a complex structure of metal and physics that she knew she'd never take the time to understand. Instead she would go through her to-do list, and brace herself for big plates of food, too-green lawns and judgmental looks as she tried to justify her presence, five years older than she had been the last time they had seen her. Before Paa Kwesi had gotten sick. That was a time when she used to make bi-yearly trips to see him and called him 'father', trying to forget all the ways he had left her and her mother when she was six years old, to discover his young American Dream. For a time, she had believed that she could forgive his leaving, if only he promised to stay in other ways. If he forged a relationship with her, albeit a long-distance one. If he didn't speak so disparagingly about her mother, whose parenting had suffered because of his own hands-off approach. As though he was not the reason she'd had to leave the house every morning of Nana's childhood at the crack of dawn to clean office buildings in Canary Wharf, before spending weekends braiding the hair of other tired mothers, just so Nana could have her choice of breakfast cereals when they went food shopping.

Now Nana could count on one hand the amount of times her mother had mentioned Paa Kwesi, as if saying his name too many times was a devastation that would end her life. So Nana learned how to say it quietly, how to discover things about him through boxes of photographs, whispers from knowing aunties and then, finally, an address. They exchanged airmail letters often, and she would greet the postman as a house guest, opening the front door as soon as she saw him coming, eager for her special delivery — and for her mother not to see. Later she realised her mother knew, as she knew most things that Nana was doing in secret. But still, the thrill of having something that was just for her and Paa Kwesi, it was unmatched for a long time. Even after the letters stopped, after she'd discovered by accident that she was a big sister, after he'd stopped calling.

The thing between them, it was fixed in her mind at a point in time when she was nine years old and her mother let her get on a plane to reach him, to meet the elusive traveller. It was a year of new things. Of a first plane ride, of eating out more in two weeks than she would ever do again in her young life, and of time spent with Paa Kwesi. Who he was and what he did, she couldn't be sure, but she remembered how he'd carried her up to bed when she fell asleep in the car, tuckered out as the jet lag hit her. Or the pride he wore on his face when he presented her with an outfit he had bought for her; an ugly one that she wished much later she'd kept for posterity, not thrown out in disgust as a teenager.

She didn't see him again for two more years, as she unknowingly became a sister for the second and third time. During her next visit, Nana saw Paa Kwesi's dream being realised, in the form of a new family. He had built a big house in the suburbs, wore polo shirts and played golf with colleagues. He belly-laughed with a cigar hanging out of his mouth at family BBQs, and he loved his children. Nana sat off to the side and wondered if she was really one of them, one of the children.

*

The seatbelt sign was switched off, and Nana flicked through the dozen or so films now available to her. She clicked on a romcom and thought about how everything came back to love, how it had to, somehow. She resented this trip happening now, at the cusp of something substantial developing with Josie. They had only just started talking about the future. She pulled out her phone and hit the PLAY button in an open WhatsApp message, a voice flooding her ears and soothing her.

Remember me, remember me, remember me under the sun.

Seinabo Sey was Nana's favourite singer, and sometimes Josie would record snippets of her songs and send them to Nana, always when she needed them most. It was a secret thing between them that Nana never wanted anyone else to know about; too sacred for others to muse over without knowing the backstory. The way their friendship had been an immediate clicking into place that still astonished Nana. How she'd been bereft when they first met, with all the ways that London life had kicked her, left her uncertain of herself, her motivations, her value. How Josie had been a silent guide, a gentle push away from the stabbing sadness that gripped Nana sometimes until she felt simultaneously comforted and trapped in a depressive swaddle. In this state, Nana would often hide for weeks at a time, burying herself in work, communicating little or nothing to any other human being, afraid she would infect them with a darkness of which she knew the full DNA. But with Josie, Nana exhaled, breathing back into life because of the softness of the arms that were opened up to her, welcoming Nana into a new moment that was filled with a kind of love she'd never, ever wondered about.

It was between Nana, Josie and those they loved; an outward step towards life with someone who helped Nana feel like a real person, almost whole. But it was not yet something she could share with blood; not with her mother, at least. And she never intended to share it with Paa Kwesi. Her life events now were a privilege, not a right. It was what she had told Josie one night, hoping she believed her own words as they vibrated in her throat.

'He doesn't get a say in anything anymore. No opinion, no right to information. That's the deal.'

The deal was with herself, when she found out he was sick. First, *what a thing to think of in response to his mortality*, and then: *this is how it is*. Their relationship hadn't started that way, but it was where they were now.

Over the years, her memories of Paa Kwesi had become shattered pieces of glass, gathered up hastily, possibly with key parts missing. The Christmas she'd spent with him mostly hiding her tears as he made small comments about her weight, her sixteen-year-old self barely able to keep her face together. The off-handed way he referred to her mother, as if she were an incubator, not the one who kept Nana alive. The big day trip to the coast, the one time Nana had felt closest to him, until they bumped into a close friend of his, who knew Paa Kwesi's family life very well.

'And you, Nana, are you a cousin or who?'

The moment still crushed her in an embarrassing way; as if she were ashamed to exist simply because her father hadn't mentioned her as his first child. She flushed and mumbled and saw that Paa Kwesi didn't really care about her discomfiture, or did not know how to. He knew how to purchase school books for her, fly her to places, buy her things. But she learned quickly that what he could afford financially and emotionally were two very different things.

Her lack of real or imagined presence in his life was publicly called out by others two or three more times before she learned the lesson. First, the questions from people Paa Kwesi named as close friends, family even, then the looking back and forth between the two of them, before the exclamation:

'Ah, Paa Kwesi! I didn't know this was your daughter, you didn't say!'

Nana was grateful for the way they were always just as confused as she, but Paa Kwesi didn't seem to find it pertinent to acknowledge her in any capacity when she wasn't standing right beside him. Her visits to his American life went quickly from often, to sometimes, to none at all.

The first time Nana distanced herself, trying to untangle the thread that stretched between the two of them and wrapped around her throat, she told him she had quit her job to pursue something he perceived to be less stable. Paa Kwesi grunted over the phone, asked her if she had really thought it through, that life wasn't about turning away from good money.

'You cannot just discard something you've put time and energy into, not when it is something that you can build up to make your life better.'

She felt like she saw him properly then, at last. His ability to discard was unmatched. She thought about it all the time. Finishing lunch and tossing out a banana skin, she thought of Paa Kwesi. When she tied up the kitchen bin, ready to take it outside, she thought of Paa Kwesi. Sometimes she got up and left Josie sleeping to watch from the window in a sleepy, anxiety-ridden haze, to think of Paa Kwesi. A light sleeper, she was too aware of outside noise, the bustle of crowds at the kebab shops on her road late at night, or the men in luminous vests early in the morning dragging loose-wheeled bins and their contents into the angry, open mouth of the rubbish truck.

She liked the way they followed a pattern of collection, the way they joked with each other sometimes, the foul smell of the truck merely a familiar scent, like dew on the ground or a smoky tang of hot tar being rolled for a new patch of road. Often Nana was tempted to open the window, call out to them, shout a thank-you for clearing the city's waste away, for dealing with the things a Londoner deemed finished with. Sometimes she fell back to sleep on the sofa, wondering what it would feel like to be inside the mouth, with other things that had been discarded.

*

The plane was mostly empty, which was to be expected. Hand sanitiser, disposable face masks, a social-distance smizing — these things had become the norm. Nana still wasn't sure she should be travelling, and even now would have been at home if Josie hadn't asked her the question, hadn't pulled her closer so that their noses touched, so that she knew Josie's words were coming from the place of love where they always originated.

'Do you think you've missed anything from him?'

It was a simple query, framed just so. Nana thought about it, inspected it, and eventually recognised the words as her own. They had been hanging on her tongue for five years. She was aware then that she felt without something, and that she had to make the trip, to reclaim whatever it was she had left with him.

Josie dropped her off before the sun had begun to crown, watching the mouthless patrons of the airport pass by the cars with their suitcases, intent on a destination, nervous about the time it would take to get there. Nana said something about it being too early in the day, in the year, in that time of the world to travel, virus prevention and all. Josie simply looked at her with a softness that made Nana want to take a nap in the back seat. They said what was a long goodbye for a distance of just two weeks. Then Nana entered the transitional structure of the terminal.

Two hours before the plane was due to make the descent to its final destination, she stared wistfully out of the window at the darkened clouds and the possibility of never really landing. Her gut was already preparing itself for a disappointing welcome, Paa Kwesi in repose, surrounded by loved ones, edging towards his final breath but still able to look her up and down disapprovingly, as if she had been the one missing for all those years.

'The prodigal daughter returns.'

She might sniff at his words, no longer afraid of the narrowing of his eyebrows, the glint of the gold watch she had never seen him without, the morsels of care he sometimes deemed to throw at her if he was in a generous mood. She was five years more than the person he had last known, and her countenance wouldn't be shaken.

'I have returned. And what have you prepared for me?'

She hoped the last word would be hers, and that perhaps the only thing she needed was to see him leave, once more.

The Nod

Joshua Idehen

I see brethren in a foreign land
we cross paths and exchange

a nod. In this kinda place where
this kinda pigment's scarce

I don't really care if brethren's
from these parts, it's enough they

exist. Cuz just this last hour past
a Berliner asked me if I sold ganja in two

languages. No one but brethren knows
how mad that is. A nod is not

a thing taught me
like a handshake or a courtesy

My first one was on an escalator
in Helsinki. I was heading up,

brethren was descending. We clocked each other
and I hadn't realised how alone I'd been, all this time

In a mall of cutting looks
upon brethren's eyes I felt seen

As brethren passed by, I would've said hi
but my pride wouldn't let me

go for a hug, maybe a hi-five,
was scared brethren wouldn't get me

But they did a nod, and without thinking
I did a nod. That's how I knew we were safe

Like all it takes is us brethren
and Helsinki is my city

us brethren and Berlin
is my backyard

us brethren and Sweden
is my mum's garden

Any other time, we would've shaken hands
taken seats at a random, politely hostile café,

chuckled at the awkward
interaction with the counter girl,

our masks off
our smiles big and bad

our language uncoded
our laughter untethered

to decorum, bullying
the premises, our voices so

loud and unbothered, like we're in
the belly of our mothers' kitchens

like we're about to fight
like we live here

Sometimes there's a nod
Sometimes there's not

Sometimes they didn't see you
Sometimes they don't see you

Sometimes they lost
Sometimes you're lost

Sometimes you're straitjacketed
in your skin, and theirs is an unfortunate disguise

so it's a blessing when we do clock
and the joy is on lock

Don't wanna gas up emotions
Don't wanna let them lot know our motions

So we keep interactions brief
Solidarity as a raised brow

Love is a hand on chest
Respect is a two-fingered salute

shot from the temple
blessings sent with a wink

Inside our smiles are whole sonnets
the ears of them lot are ignorant to

We're comets
passing through a clouded night,

we're needles in a haystack state
where the god of the land don't know our face

And the law of the land's like 'know your place'
But look at that, we've found each other, so we must be safe

How amazing is this? Are we not alive?
Is that not a good thing?

Bodies

Translated from the Bengali by Selina Parveen Rahman and the author

Shagufta Sharmeen Tania

It was an intolerably hot morning in July on the day that Fancy and Nancy's youngest uncle, standing for a long time in his room, went crazy. He'd been standing in the middle of the room for a very long time. Possibly since the night before.

Fancy attended music school; Nancy, dance school. Fancy practised the harmonium for an hour every morning. She started with classical music and then gradually moved to Tagore songs, following the notations.

That morning, when Fancy had just reached that line of the Tagore song where the river pulses exuberantly, her youngest uncle saw the glowing hot sun turn into a white ball of snow that never turned golden again. The maid came into the room to find Fancy's uncle standing in the middle of the room muttering to himself, wearing Fancy's mother's sari.

It should be mentioned at this point that Fancy's youngest uncle had a name — a formal name and a pseudonym. He used the pseudonym to write for newspapers and magazines. One day, the postman delivered a letter addressed to 'Twigs of Parijata'. It was good that Fancy's grandfather had already passed away; otherwise he'd have thrashed Fancy's youngest uncle with his wooden sabots for giving away his Muslim name.

Okay, Fancy's youngest uncle's name was Shah Alam, named after the last Mughal emperor whose empire was increasingly decimated until it could be squeezed between Delhi and Palam village! His nickname was 'Dilu'. The maid who found him in his mad state was Parul Begum, a level-headed woman; her way of doing things was meticulous and her work, generally, was immaculate. She was the one to call the compounder, Nurul, the local doctor's assistant. Now, Nurul only knew how to administer injections. He became nervous when he saw the condition of Fancy's uncle, who was crawling around the room. It was Parul's idea to lock Fancy's uncle in the attic for the time being.

Fancy and Nancy skipped school that day. Manju, their mother, had been planning to see the movie *Durdesh* with the landlord's son. She had to cancel her plans. The girls' father was arriving in the second week of the next month anyway, so Manju didn't place a long-distance call to inform him.

Dilu remained locked in the attic until his older brother arrived. The rooftop was a place very close to Dilu's heart. Mango slices were sun-baked there, as were jars of seasonal pickles and preserved lemons. Indian jasmine blossomed in harmony with vegetables such as okra and herby perennials. Madagascan periwinkles would sometimes bloom along the cornice, their flowers as purple as the evening sky. Dilu had a habit of perambulating around the rooftop and memorising his lessons, amusing himself as to why Carolus Linnaeus had named a certain flower *Clitoria*. He was a student of botany. Pranksome Manju would fly kites bought by Dilu in the autumn; Fancy would sing film songs and Nancy would dance. In the winter, Parul would make rice-flour patties on a makeshift earthen stove. All on that rooftop. We'll never know how Dilu felt in his state of amnesia, locked in the rooftop room that had once been a haven of happy and joyful memories! There's no way to know.

By the time her father arrived, Fancy had learned a whole new Nazrul song. Dilu's older brother arrived from Bahrain with lots of gifts and commodities. Demonstrating a steady nerve, he promptly admitted Dilu into a rehabilitation centre in Mirpur. There Dilu picked up the habit of smoking, kept himself busy digging the garden looking for hidden treasure and believed that the man in the next bed had been driven mad by his conspiring wife, who'd fed him the meat of a vulture. Dilu fitted in fine there!

Manju spent the days cooking her husband's favourite dishes: fried chapila fish, lentil with jute leaves and roasted pigeon. Over the years, her husband had become healthier. Manju hadn't liked him at all when they'd married. She had sparkling eyes and long, beautiful hair, like a princess in a fairy tale. This man with termite-riddled health, clad in oversized clothes, looked no match for her! But she accepted him calmly, in the same manner one accepts one's own name, parents' faces, siblings, birth identity. She accepted it all: the husband, his habits, his life in a foreign land, the twins. The lonely afternoons were filled with the cawing of crows and Fancy's plaintive numbers; they were spent standing at the window or preparing kites, the strings sharpened by a mix of ground-up lightbulbs and rice gruel. Until her husband returned, that's how her placid, waveless afternoons passed.

Was it really that doleful? Manju's boundless energy, her striking physicality and her scandalous frivolity overflowed through the house. Dilu, her bosom buddy, would say, 'You're no animal, you're a plant — a climber. If pruned on one side, you start growing from the other. You need a Latin nomenclature bestowed on you!' Manju would just laugh it away. She somehow knew that her manners were not very malleable, and that her motherhood lacked grammar! She had to pay the price for that.

Dilu's older brother was the sort of everyman who can be seen all over the place — at a bus stop, at the post office, on a ferry, at a teahouse or launderette; an ordinary man who didn't pose any surprises, a man who is both scared of, and hungry for, a beautiful female body. So Manju was loved by him only during sex. The rest of the time, he controlled her through his injunctions. In other words, it would be untrue to say that Manju counted the days till her husband's return. She spent her time in harmony with the ever-so-friendly Dilu, soulmate Parul and, to some extent, her twin daughters. She never became aware of her shortcomings as a wife. She was not very adept at household chores, and though her cooking wasn't inedible, it wasn't out of this world either. In fact, the cooking was mainly done by Parul. Her daughters stayed in their school uniforms after school; they wore blue slips under pink frocks ... and all this would go unnoticed by their mother. She heard Nancy grinding her teeth in her sleep, but would forget to send Parul for de-worming medicine in the morning.

You might assume that Manju wrote poetry in stealth, or that she was an ardent singer who had given up singing after marriage. Unfortunately, Manju had no mysterious past; she had no undiscovered potential, nor was she ruined. She was what she was — open wide, unashamedly healthy. Born free like the grass spikelet, undifferentiated and graceless! Manju had been married off just before her school SSC exams. Her husband had toyed with her for a bit, sighed, then left for Bahrain. During the ensuing exam fever, Manju came to her in-laws' house to nurse her dying mother-in-law. Enthusiastic Dilu helped her solve the test papers for a while, composed essays such as 'A Monsoon Evening' for her to memorise, and wrote with the exam biros to get them ready for intellectual proliferation. All his preparations were in vain; Manju failed English, and discovered that she was pregnant. That's all there is to know about Manju.

We can't tell whether her surging restlessness also echoed inside Dilu's heart at times, whether the poet 'Twigs of Parijata' felt inspired to compose a lyric for Manju. Manju would be restless with fear when she received a letter from her expat husband, as if she had received a summons from court. Her handwriting was terrible, her sense of spelling almost primitive. Interestingly enough, it was Dilu who would write the replies to those letters, quoting from Tagore's poems. Manju would laugh to death ... Bahrain would only sigh!

By now, I believe you recognise that Manju was the stage actress of the drama. Parul Begum was the cook who conjured roasted pigeon in the background; Dilu, the writer working on her behalf in the green room; Dilu's older brother, a husband denied any personal touch from the wife.

Let's look at Dilu now. Let's see how trapped he was in a cocoon, on his journey to becoming 'Twigs of Parijata'. Dilu was everybody's pal, noiseless, bottomless and timid. He made milkmaid braids out of his nieces' hair and wrote love letters to his elder brother. During the holidays, he got wood-apple chutney for the women in the house. He accompanied Parul to and from her village home in Gafargaon. And flew kites with Manju.

Dilu sincerely loved his older brother. At night, in his room, he would overhear him cooling himself with a palm-leaf fan and narrating how orange-flower lemonade and rosewater-boiled meat garnished with ruby-like pomegranate beads were served in Bahrain. Dilu certainly knew that Manju was paying little attention to those elaborate culinary details told by a starving worker from the Middle East. She might be picking her teeth with a safety pin and dozing off. Dilu was almost suffocated by love for his brother in the dark.

In rehab, Dilu nursed everyone. He brought water to those who woke up in the dead of night, embraced jilted men crying over the betrayals of their beloveds, shared the fruit his brother brought during visits, mended the shirts and sewed on the torn buttons of fighting inmates. The man whose wife had fed him a dead vulture needed to be in chains. He would describe the body of his wife and, although Dilu felt shy, he would listen to the depiction lest the man feel hurt.

Beyond the barbed-wire fences, there was fallow land and dusty earth, the round sky tipped over like a blue glass bowl, a slender date palm and Asian fig trees that looked as if testicles grew on their trunks. On sunny days the wild smell and bluebottles from those fields entered Dilu's window. Did all that came through the window make 'Twigs of Parijata' emotional? Did it bring back the memory of Parul's fig and onion curry? Or perhaps he just listlessly listened to the detailed description of an unseen woman's breasts...

Dilu's older brother remained depressed during his vacation. He didn't discipline the girls while checking on their schoolwork. Wearing his gold-coloured suit, he left as soon as the vacation was over. Manju was not exactly unaffected by this! For the first time she felt alone, unsheltered, friendless and surrounded by hostilities. The girls made silly poems – 'Make a face and eat a frog/Drown and die in the bog' – and broke out in laughter. Manju became irritated by the noise. The evening sky turned orange-red like a pomegranate, and made her cry. The tabloids, with pictures of voluptuous heroines, remained open but unattended. Things were falling apart.

Parul called Fancy and Nancy and told them that the family was going through a period of crisis and that the twins had to remember the lessons they'd received as recent recruits to the Yellow Birds girl guides. Parul reminded them of the details she'd overheard from the girls themselves: that they were promise-bound to fulfil their duties towards God and country, to help others and, especially, to help their mother in her daily chores. The girls soon started handpicking husks and stones from the rice in the kitchen and pulling out Parul's grey hairs.

Subsequently, Manju discovered that she was pregnant. She remembered how Dilu had taken care of her when she'd been pregnant with the twins. Whatever she'd craved – piquant green tomatoes, tamarind, ice cream – Dilu would get it for her. Manju started crying like a motherless daughter. The twins were so moved by this display of sorrow that they scurried to do more household chores.

The days of pregnancy were idle. Manju watched Hindi movies on the new VCR. She loved to watch TV, that box that displayed an eternal spring, everlasting roses in gardens, dancing maids in glittering outfits. By the time Fancy had learned to play a new song and Nancy had learned to dance to it, Manju had gone to Farida Clinic and come back carrying a swaddled little boy. For the first time in her life, she sat down to write a letter to her husband without Dilu's help. Her husband had always wanted a boy. But he wasn't surprised by the news. Many times, in his deepest thoughts, or in a blabbering state of drunkenness, or while merely suffering from flu, he'd nurtured this possibility.

That autumn, many a brown-paper-coloured moth fluttered on the windowpanes. The cold wind carried the advent of winter. Parul Begum was about to prepare rice-flour patties.

Manju was scrubbing the baby with mustard oil. Her twins needed to be scrubbed with hot-sticky grease from coconut balls that made babies hairless. Boys didn't need that treatment. A short splash of rain had left some mist in the air; the sun shone on the treetops and the glittering dome of the mosque. Autumn insects covered the walls. Manju's little son was cooing like a dove. The neighbours were burning frankincense as their evening ritual; it repelled the mosquitos, but irritated Manju's eyes.

On such an evening, Manju's husband arrived without any notice.

A wave of happiness swept throughout the house, Fancy and Nancy started screaming in excitement. Their father brought a lot of gifts for them: dolls, chocolates, dresses. Their baby brother also mumbled sounds of gratification, so as to join in the festivity. Manju dressed up her son. Her husband sat in silence for a long time with his new-born son in his arms, whispering, 'My son!'

Parul started cooking pilao rice, and Manju changed into a sari with a golden border and came to help her in the kitchen. Parul giggled and said the man was beyond joy to father a son: 'He's as stunned as if struck by thunder!'

The real lightning actually struck in the early morning, inside the mosquito net. Manju's husband started muttering to himself, semi-audibly: 'A (…) woman who goes to her brother-in-law to hatch eggs, she belongs in (…), he was no man to fall into the trap of such a (…) woman, when did her (…) become insane? And when did she become pregnant with this (…) child?'

Manju couldn't fathom what was really happening. She kept staring at her husband like a fool looking at difficult spelling. Suddenly she remembered that she'd cooked pilao rice for her husband, put on make-up, become intimate with him in bed at night. Even when her husband flew into a rage and started beating her, she remained as if under ether, at one remove from the humiliation.

Let's move from this room to the other. Fancy and Nancy are trembling in fear, hugging Parul Begum's bosom. There's not much to see there except some old magazines, tattered quilts, paperchains from an old birthday party.

Let's move from this house to another, let's time-travel to about a year ago in the past. We see Dilu giving tuition to his student Shelly in a small room, the usual props in evidence: the essay book by Haralal Roy, teacups and some snacks, a chit inside the book, some dry flowers between the sheets. We see Dilu and Shelly in the same room, unchaperoned again, on another day. Shelly's face glows like phosphorus; Dilu's face suddenly awakens from a deep state of love, his whole body swaying like a pendulum as he stands there in shock and fear while Shelley slaps him hard on the face. Dilu is trying come to terms with the fact that he is impotent, unable to have an erection.

Let's move from this country and cross the oceans to enter Dilu's older brother's room. How hard he works as a driver in Bahrain. We may see a woman, a regular visitor to this room for years, lying on his bed — it must be the mother of the girl who'd slept in his bed a few hours back. They looked like pearly Venuses sprung out of the shell. They had the blood of the Bedouin in their veins, and eyes of gazelles. Can you imagine how difficult it was to service both of them — and their car? Or we may see that Dilu's older brother had already eloped with his employer's daughter, long before Manju became pregnant or Dilu turned mad. Today, Dilu's older brother would return from Bangladesh to his Bedouin wife.

Let's move a bit above. Under the everlasting deep blue sky of the desert, the Bedouin woman is changing the direction of her tent after divorcing her husband. She'd position it towards the south if it had been northwards before. If it were eastwards, it would be turned westwards now. This indicated divorce. This was the rule of the land. The desert land.

III friends

'It's the optimism that's the worst.'

AND Keep that Lighter Burning...

Jamie Thrasivoulou

AND watched them load their memories of this Promised Land into the back of a Transit van. It was too much, so escaped reality through backstreet boozer saloon door; entered the Promised Land in nanoseconds, arrived AND present — Liverpool thrashing City on the telly. Jed, the *true Brit* is hosting an angry post-work barstool summit; judgement slammed down, Carling-glass-clang on wood. – *Got some cheek them lot, summat not quite right about that – could be carrying bodies or drugs or owt, look at the state of 'em – not quite right!* The glare from a headlight skims the Romanian number plate. AND watched through the window, watched the family load nowt to write home about into a self-addressed envelope. AND now there's a few of Jed's cronies at it, dishing out the *banter*, serving it up with all the sauce AND trimmings. Then there's a goal AND the summit loses momentum; the convo turns to Derby-born men arguing over falsified allegiances – *there's notter Manc or Scouser in the building – so pipe it down you pair!* Jed's not losing this one, oh no, he's not losing this one, eyes bulged towards the window once more; – *Just who do they think they are, just who do they think they are? It's really not right.* AND watched Jed's blood boil to a chemical crescendo, mouth-frothed, teeth chopping like a guillotine. AND off to the bogs for a leveller; reappears with a ring of confidence. Necks that Carling gas AND he's outside; Jed is outside the building, for a fag … AND the streetlights pan to a young Romanian lad, asking Jed for a lighter: *light please sir, light please sir?* Jed obliges; sure he does, lands him a *good 'en* – *ha-ha-ha*, AND watches gob flobbed right across the youth's brow. AND then Jed is down, Jed is down AND out of the building AND waking up with a crowd around him. AND there is more laughter than tears AND I'm just watching, I'm just watching him come round whilst passing the young Romanian lad a lighter AND telling him — he can keep it.

I = You

Ashleigh Nugent

I understand that you won't understand
'cause you could never live as me –
but I know what you think
'cause I am you.

You aspire to be John Wayne
or Winston Churchill or the Queen,
to win the Crown or win a war
or slaughter folks at Wounded Knee.
And when we grew and learned
our heroes saw my family as the enemy,
well, you could just forget such facts
'cause you could never live as me.

We had the biggest empire:
your White, their red and blue.
We are the cleverest, the bravest
and most worthy – point is proved.
But when it dawned on us –
the blood we drink is how the empire grew!
It was easier to ignore the guilt,
I know 'cause I am you.

When they say muddy-coloured people
are polluting our White country,
and there's something in their blood
that makes them indolent and ugly,
you don't have to sift the ashes
of your old identity
to understand how you agreed with them
'cause you could never live as me.

Obama changed the narrative
so now, what we accrue
is all attributive to what the
individual may choose.
Institutions, Trump, and history
are easy to refute.
You want to think that we're all colour-blind;
I know, 'cause I am you

You will never feel that everything
you say and do and be
is being observed and compared
and judged uncompromisingly,
and deemed innate to all who shared your shade
throughout all human history.
This burden's never crossed your mind,
'cause you could never live as me.

And logic seems to state
that if 'we' gain, 'you' surely lose,
even if the only gain was
some brief mention in the news,
or a few flimsy attempts
to be more honest in their schools.
But if I truly gain it's your gain too
I know, 'cause I am 'me' and 'you'.

So stop and think. Get real!
This thing is nowhere near through.
Don't doubt you have my love, though;
you should know 'cause I am you
and I will stop, and feel, and understand
that blame won't help us breathe.
And I will speak. But will you listen?
Because you could never live as me.

Olden Friends Are Golden

Tabish Khair

Giridhar sat in a wicker chair on the balcony of his palatial new house in a suburb of Bhopal, and browsed through the seven daily newspapers, three in Hindi, to which he subscribed. It was seven-thirty in the morning. He had been up from five-thirty, as was his routine: first his puja, then yoga and a stint on his exercise bike before taking a shower in cold water, for that was good for his circulation. Now he had exactly half an hour on his own before the business of the day began: seeing people. Giridhar was a municipal councillor, hoping to get a ticket from the Congress Party to become a Member of the Legislative Assembly. He had retired early as a police officer to enter this field.

His wife walked in with a tray. On it were a cup of tea and a plate with two arrowroot biscuits. She put it on the wicker table and went back into the house to instruct the cook. Breakfast had to be served exactly at eight. One of the three smartphones on the table buzzed. Giridhar looked at it with annoyance; this was his private moment. Then he saw it was a message from the WhatsApp group he shared with his old school friends from Phansa, a small town in another state. He picked up the phone.

Lakshmi had finished supervising her husband's office-going rituals. His office was in another part of the house. What he did there was partly a mystery to Lakshmi. One part of it. The part that had to do with making money. The money that had enabled them to move out of Phansa and buy this sprawling farmhouse outside Lucknow. The other part she knew and understood. Her husband wrote historical novels. He published them under his own imprint, because established publishers were so biased. But since 2014, her husband had started receiving prizes and attention. The prizes were by organisations with names like the Hindu Renewal League or Sanatana Dharma Sahitya or the Yogi Trading Association, not the Booker Committee or even the Sahitya Akademi, but Lakshmi was not familiar with the distinction between such organisations. The prizes showered on her husband seemed impressive to her, and the functions involved ministers, dozens of impassive-looking people, sometimes even TV and film stars. Just last year, when they had finally visited the USA, her husband had been honoured as a 'bestselling author' at a literary event organised by the Indian High Commission. Lakshmi was happy with her life – she designed dresses in her spare time – and proud of her husband. She devoted full attention to him when he was around. But the moment he left – a pile of books carried behind him by a servant – she picked up her iPhone. That is when she saw the WhatsApp message.

Santosh saw the message at eight in the company bus that he took to work. Even though he had a car, this was Delhi. He did not want to drive needlessly and could not afford a driver. Or, actually, he *could* afford a driver, if only drivers were not such cheats, because the last one had not only asked for repeated rises, but had also siphoned off and sold petrol from the tanks of his Hyundai i20. There was no point. The corporation he worked for ran company buses, and it took just thirty to forty minutes, an hour if the traffic was bad, so Santosh mostly left his car behind. It also enabled him to catch up on office gossip in the air-conditioned bus and check his iPhone, for, unlike the other men he knew, Santosh was a progressive person and actually helped prepare breakfast and his three children for school, after which both he and his wife left for work. His wife taught in a kindergarten in the neighbourhood.

Manish had a flight to Kolkata. He was at Patna airport, which was far too small for the city. To think that when he was growing up in nearby Phansa, he had considered this a metropolis! Years of innocence. The Air India flight was forty-five minutes late. But now it had been announced and they were being called to board. He was not worried about being late. Manish was high enough in the multi-layered Life Insurance

Corporation for people to wait for his arrival. As he walked to the gate, he felt his iPhone buzzing in his jacket pocket. He had it on silent mode. Manish took it out and switched it off without looking at the messages. It was his policy never to check anything on his mobile phone while boarding a plane. The last time he had done so, about a decade ago in 2008, there had been news of a share market collapse that had cost him more than four lakhs before his plane had finally landed and he could sell off his shares. It had been the worst flight of his life. He would switch on his iPhone only when he landed. What happens, happens.

Sunita almost missed the message. She had left in a rush for her work at a private Bangalore college – having finally managed to get tenure at the age of forty-nine, just six years ago – and by the time she took her lunch break in the college cafeteria, so many messages had piled up that she could not even look at all of them. But then a colleague in the cafeteria remarked: 'Olden friends are golden.' It reminded her that she had not checked her old school WhatsApp group for a day or two now. She could see twenty-one unread messages highlighted there. The number jumped out at her. Some were from yesterday. But most were from the morning. They were all in response to a message by Arjun that had been posted early in the morning, at 7:32 exactly. Arjun was the only person from the group who was still in Phansa, the town where they had all grown up and whose best English-medium school they had attended. Six boys and girls (out of a graduation batch of twenty-three) had stayed on in town. They did not connect to the WhatsApp group: one boy had died of alcoholism, though no one talked about it, and two were struggling financially; another boy, always a loner, was said to be depressed; and the two girls who had been married early into families in the town claimed they were not on WhatsApp. Arjun ran a successful clothes retailing business in Phansa and was the only one in the group. He was their source of news from their old hometown.

Akbar had two iPhones: one for work/family and one for fun. He never looked at the latter until his lunch break well after two, depending on when he'd finished examining all the files and orders piled up on his desk, as well as the previous day's productivity charts for the eleven employees in his export–import business in Ahmedabad. The old school WhatsApp group was obviously on his 'fun' iPhone, and he saw the message only when he switched it on at 3:07. It had been a busy day. The last message was from Adarsh. This was rare. Adarsh was the only one from the batch to become a doctor; he had moved to the USA and seldom participated in the group chats that erupted abruptly every few days. Akbar read the conversation carefully. He frowned. He read it again. He wondered if he should reply. It was a difficult choice. He felt he should say something. But he hesitated.

Arjun

I thought I should inform you that Aurangzeb's brother has left for Pakistan. Local police investigating his family here. National security issue. His parents interrogated. I was told this morning. It all took place last night. You know Aurangzeb had been arrested before he left for London ten years ago... Very worrying developments. For all of us.

7:32

Giridhar

Calm down, dost. I have been in the police. Aurangzeb was arrested for some street protest, nothing devastating. People leaving for Pakistan is not a national security issue. No one's parent interrogated for that let me assure you. Been there done that

7:35

Arjun
Giridhar Babu you might know but I do not know anyone who has left for Pakistan. I am quoting reliable sources. Believe not beleive

7:36

Giridhar
What? Dost dost na raha? Of course believe you Guru, but sources please? ☺

7:37

Arjun
Reliable. Cannot reveal name for obvious reasons

7:40

Lakshmi
Oh God! We do not need this. I did not even know Aurangzeb was in this group. He was trouble even in school. It was lucky he was not rusticated. Who put him on? Who else has been sneaked into this group? This is beyond belief! This is a private group.

8.03

Giridhar
Guru Arjun, do not give me all that classified stuff... I have been an officer. ☺

8:34

Arjun

Giridhar Babu, not everyone flies as high as you or your precious Lutyen Congress does. I have been told by sources that anyone corresponding with Aurangzeb or his family will be under surveillance. Lakshmi ji, I think Sudeep put Aurangzeb on.

8:41

Lakshmi

Sudeep!!!? He left us in class seven! Why is HE in the group? I have seen no posting from him or Aurangzeb anyway. Why are they here if they do not post? What is the point? Why are there so many people here who do not post? MANISH, did you make Sudeep the coordinator? I thought you were the coordinator? Who did this? Oh my God, my husband will be so upset. He knows all these government high-ups... We had dinner with a state minister just last Saturday.

8:42

Arjun

I agree this is looking bad, friends.

8:46

Sudeep

Lakshmi ji, your husband was in touch with Aurangzeb just a year ago, when he wanted some books to be shipped over from London. I know. Aurangzeb told me, he went to a library for the first time since college to order photocopies of the three books... So, if you excuse my Sanskrit: wtf?

10:48

Lakshmi
I am not talking to you, Sudeep ji. I hardly remember you from school. You left for another school, when, in class seven? This is a group for people who graduated together, as far as I am concerned. I am asking Manish. MANISH, where are you? I am going to call you on the phone now. This needs to be sorted out. You stay out of this, Sudeep ji.

10:53

Arjun
Sudeep Babu, this is serious. I will be leaving the group if Aurangzeb continues to be part of it. I have no desire to associate with people being investigated by the authorities. His brother was interviewed by security at the airport I have it from reliable sources. I think some of us will have to leave as we do not live in liberal metropolitan circles you know

10:57

Giridhar
Take is easy, Guru. It means nothing. Who are your sources?

11:06

Sunita
Oh no, I just saw this. I am shocked. Aurangzeb has been in London for years. Didn't he graduate from Aligarh Muslim University?

12:16

Arjun
Yes. His brother was a student leader there too.

12:18

Lakshmi

I finally got in touch with Manish. He was on a flight. He is going to delete Aurangzeb as soon as he gets home. We cannot have the police looking into our group. Not that we have anything to hide, but we want to be free to talk about our lives and common experiences. We do not want to be watched. You should not have connected him, Sudeep ji. It was very immature of you. You knew his background. It is not as if he is like Akbar: he was always a trouble-maker.

12:47

Sudeep left.

Sunita

I do not understand what is up. Why did Sudeep leave?

12:53

Santosh

Just saw this. Are we sure about all this? I mean Aurangzeb was a bit wild, and so was his brother, I guess, but I recall him drinking beer with us. Not really the Pakistani type, if you ask me...

1:21

Giridhar

Guru Santosh, who can doubt Arjun Guru's sources? ;-)

1:25

Arjun

Thank you Giridhar Boss. That is good coming from you and your party...;-)

1:56

Manish

Doing it in five minutes, if no objections. Sorry for the hassle, friends. Let's all just stay calm. OK?

2:01

Aurangzeb removed

Santosh

I still think we should have given Aurangzeb time to respond. Maybe he would have clarified? Just saying. ☺

2:03

Sunita

Well, he did get time from 7:30 this morning. I do not like this, but why didn't he clarify? It is unfair to do this to your school friends. We all have our own lives, our own troubles. I know my college-board... They do not want people with controversies teaching in college. Jobs do not sit on branches for some of us...

2:08

Giridhar

Perhaps because England is about four five hours behind us, Sunita ji? Not that I have been there... ☺

2:13

Lakshmi

We have to be careful who we allow into this group. It has to be close friends. People we know. People we can trust. These are dangerous times. Did you read about the ISI agents arrested just two weeks ago?

2:13

Santosh

Oh well, what is done is done. Arjun, now don't you leave too!!!

2:13

Adarsh

What's up? Where is Arjun going????

3:07

Manish

Yes, Arjun, stay on, yaar. Let's not break old ties.

3:15

Adarsh

Sorry friends. Just got up. Have read it now. Sad. Sad. Never thought… But Arjun, don't leave…

3:18

Arjun

No reason for anyone to leave now. Yes, Adarsh Boss, very sad.

4:06

Giridhar

Attaboy! Ye yaari hum nahin todeingey…

4:15

Lakshmi

Sudeep should have thought about this. Just put us in a spot, without thinking. Selfish of him. So relieved things are getting back to normal.

4:17

> **Sunita**
> Great you are staying Arjun. You are our man in Phansa.
> And olden friends are golden.
>
> 4:19

> **Lakshmi**
> I just had this idea, friends. Why don't we make a shared
> online album of photos from our high school years? I
> have quite a few. Should I do it, and then give access to
> you all to post photos? Nothing like school days...
>
> 4:21

> **Giridhar**
> Good idea, Lakshmi ji.
>
> 4:27

> **Sunita**
> Why didn't we think of this earlier? Great idea! Wow,
> Lakshmi you are the creative one here!
>
> 4:27

New shared album created

Akbar sits down to dinner with his two children. His wife is still in the kitchen making roti. He has been thinking about this all day, ever since he first read the messages during his late lunch break. He has seen it unfold on WhatsApp. He has hesitated half a day. But looking at his children, he feels he has to respond. Not to write anything seems worse than writing something! He takes out his 'fun' phone and keys in his message quickly, before his wife comes out with the food and tells him not to work, at least not at dinnertime...

Akbar

Hey, friends! What's up? Having dinner here. It has been a very busy day at work. That GST bureaucratic shit means even more work for us businessmen. I have not been able to follow anything online for days. Giridhar Bhai, you want to change professions? I am told you only sit in your office for three hours every morning! Gotta run now, guys, steaming roti on the way…

9:39

Airhead

Helen Mort

When Libra gets to the cocktail party, she digs
into her pleather handbag for her gift

and finds she's only brought the stars,
crumbled blue cheese, ash stink of them.

She excuses herself, floats to the bathroom,
locks the door, but the window's open

and her mother the sky slips in
to spy on her, criticise her sun-coloured blouse,

her loud blonde hair. Libra always has clean socks,
irons her underwear, but no one cares.

She haunts the edges of the room,
troubled by her moony face

in the flicker of a lifted wine glass, or held
in the lens of someone else's eyes.

She cannot leave a conversation
so she talks until tight smiles

become excuses, gazes drift over her shoulder.
Would you dance with her? In your arms,

she'd cleave to your shape, merge with your shadow.
She's so polite but she weighs herself down

with empty bottles, gold fizzing liquid,
hoping to anchor the kite of her heart.

So eager. It's not her fault she smells of old clouds
and aeroplane trails. Would you hold

her hand? Would you take her home
if you thought she wrote this?

Tim Wells

What Life Serves

It's cold out, and warm in. The caff windows are steamed up,
this claustrophobia pulls close. Opposite, Amar has seen off
a full English. No bacon, extra sausage. There're lines we cross,
but only so far. He takes out his phone and photos his empty
plate, still swirled with sauce. I look on, puzzled. Amar looks
up and smiles: 'It's just not right to send a picture of a full plate
of food to my mum. She's still a refugee. But an empty one,
well, she knows I'm okay.'

Why the Barmaid Is in Therapy

It's the mid-afternoons that drag. The early promise of the day
is wasted and it's the same old ruddy faces.
It's not even that they're bad people, it's just blokes like me,
we don't do therapy. She's heard it all: the job, wife, kids, team.
Her keeping that grin takes more than the odd gin.
Cleaning the glasses and bottling never stops, but at least
there's a sparkle to a glass. What's in the bottle *might* be a good
        time.
But this ain't the young crowd of an evening, this is the
        relentless
tick of the clock, rattle of prescription medication, self-reflection
in the mirror where you know not to catch anyone's eye.
It's the optimism that's the worst. It always starts so well:
'Cheers,' a bit of a joke; from thereon, the glass is half-empty.

IV work

'I didn't waste time. Four shots. Four down.'

The Invitation

Colin Grant

The BBC, as a bastion of British culture, maintains and promotes an ennobling idea of public service broadcasting that stretches beyond these shores. My invitation to join the corporation in 1991 marked a milestone for our family; it meant that we'd breached a forbidding fortress which, in the past, we'd only been able to stare at in wonderment. We could never have contemplated traversing the invisible moat or *cordon sanitaire* designed to keep the likes of us most definitely on the outside.

It wasn't just that the BBC was, in the parlance of psychologists, a 'white space' (back then we'd just say it was a 'white people ting'); it was also a compromised and compromising space. In order to get into it, you'd have to consider the possibility of debasing yourself by entering a world which, as well as soberly, conscientiously and impartially broadcasting world news, also entertained viewers on Saturday nights with *The Black and White Minstrel Show*, featuring white men with shoe-polished black faces and bowler hats dancing with long-legged white women. This really happened, on prime-time BBC 1 TV, all the way up to 1978.

A dozen years later, I was among the recruits to the BBC World Service at Bush House, passing through the portico bearing the inscription *To the Friendship of English-speaking Peoples*. First we were given a tour of the magnificent Neoclassical building and then ushered into a room and sat down for 'the talk', a rite of passage where you submitted to the notion that, as an ambassador for the BBC, you'd never ever bring the corporation into disrepute, and you'd also religiously adhere to the mantra, 'accuracy, accuracy, accuracy'. The BBC high command clearly admitted without any discomfort that, as the World Service was funded by the Foreign Office, the corporation was a clever tool in the country's soft-power strategy. Britain's governments, whomever they were led by, took vicarious pleasure in the BBC, and were rewarded in unquantifiable ways for their association with it.

Mentioning the World Service abroad in the 1990s gave you smooth entry into the lives of others; it appeared to be a kind of lingua franca or password. But, growing up in a West Indian household in Luton in the 1960s, I'd never heard of it. The first time I became aware of the World Service's existence was in a *Guardian* advert for the radio traineeship I applied for in 1989.

The advert suggested that the World Service required more employees of colour in its editorial departments. This was underlined by a little black-and-white sketch that showed two people – a man in a kente-cloth outfit and a woman in a sari – sat opposite each other at a round desk with a globe in the middle of it, giving off flashes of radio waves. Notwithstanding the cartoon's clumsiness, I was impressed by the corporation's realisation that its whiteness implied that the BBC World Service was stuck in some not-too-distant imperial past; I was glad to meet with their approval at the interview and accepted the invitation to join.

Since that invitation from the BBC, I have received five others — the last one encouraging me to take the golden handshake of redundancy and leave through the very doors I'd come in by. The other four invitations were not so attractive.

Two years ago, I left the BBC like a prisoner on a life sentence who had done his time without parole at a maximum-security detention centre. That sounds a little melodramatic, I know. There was no gangster's moll waiting for me on the outside with the engine of a Bentley running, but I did have an overwhelming sense of freedom. During my twenty-five-year career at the BBC, I'd topped the charts for being the employee with the highest number of disciplinary hearings in the corporation's history. One hearing, you might think, to paraphrase Oscar Wilde, might be regarded as a misfortune, but four smacks of carelessness.

The disciplinary hearing process and protocols were rather quaint. A booklet, outlining what to expect now that I'd been identified as a suspect, accompanied a letter that began: 'Dear Colin, I'm inviting you to a disciplinary hearing...'. The use of the word 'invite' seemed ironic, for this was not an invitation you could refuse.

All the disciplinaries were pretty ridiculous, but the third hearing strikes me as the worst. On receipt of that particular invitation – I'd been accused of acting aggressively towards a manager – I immediately phoned and left a message for the sender, a senior manager (the manager's manager, let's call him 'The Man') who, I'd later discover, would act on her behalf as the plaintiff; he'd also volunteer himself to be the chief prosecutor and, for good measure, the judge as well. But all that was in the future; for now, we were still within the realm of possibility to resolve the situation locally. The Man rang me back at my desk. It was an open-plan office. I whispered down the line that there must have been a terrible mistake. I was friendly and unaggressive, as my colleagues would attest.

The Man let me speak on and on, without interruption. Finally, I suggested to him that perhaps we could go for a drink in the bar and sort it out over a pint. There was a pause before he answered: 'No, I don't think that's right. I wouldn't want you to say anything to compromise your case.' I detected glee in his voice.

It was at that moment I realised that I wasn't quite right for the BBC (actually, I'd felt it after the first 'disciplinary', but had somehow forgotten). For the first stage of the hearing, the Man appointed a stony-faced 'impartial' investigator with experience in 'matters of race relations'.

'What three words best describe you?' asked the investigator.

I didn't care for the question — introduced, she had said, as an opening gambit, 'Just to get things started.'

'Tall and black,' I answered, straining and failing to curb a sarcastic tongue.

'And?' She persisted. 'A third word?'

'I'm not playing this game.'

'Tall, yes. Black, yes.' She spoke as a teacher might when encouraging a child with a limited vocabulary. 'And?'

'Just tall and black.'

'And aggressive? Would that be a fair description, "aggressive"?'

I didn't respond. She tried again. 'Are you surprised to hear you've been described as aggressive?'

'No.'

The investigator sat forward. 'No? You're not surprised?'

'No.'

'She says she felt you were being aggressive towards her.'

'I wasn't.'

'Yes, but she felt you were. If she felt, genuinely *felt* you to be aggressive, then you were, weren't you? Weren't you?'

I struggled with the investigator's logic, with her knight's-move thinking. But more than being confused by it, I resented it. And I was suddenly aware, in a way that I hadn't been before, that the woman from HR who sat beside the investigator was making notes. Her pen, poised above the paper, now paused.

'Take your time,' said the investigator. 'Think carefully.'

I did think, and the more I did so, the more discursive I became. I did myself no favours by objecting to the remit of the hearing and the use of the word 'aggressive' as a suitable descriptor for me. For too long, I argued, that word had been levelled at all black people. It was part of the code to keep us in our place.

'If I had been tall, white and Oxbridge-educated, you'd say I was assertive. I'll accept "assertive". But "aggressive"? No.'

My inquisitor nodded. 'So you are accusing your manager of being racist, is that right?'

As well as being investigated for my aggression, she now spelled out that they'd also be considering my allegation of racism.

'But I haven't made any such allegation,' I answered.

'This is a serious matter,' said the investigator. 'We take such accusations very seriously. It could have serious consequences for the person in question.'

'But I haven't made any accusations.'

'So you're withdrawing your complaint?'

'There was no complaint.'

The investigator seemed to brighten. 'Yes, right then, we'll consider it withdrawn,' she said, and directed the silent note-taker to strike my non-allegation from the records.

This would be the tone throughout the weeks and months of the hearing, which was already beginning to feel like a trial. As the trial progressed – every employee who'd worked with me in the past five years was asked their opinion of my character – other incidents of my alleged aggressive behaviour were put forward for consideration.

I had been naïve. I had assumed that the difficulty of getting into the BBC was the main problem, but that once you were in, then you had 'gone clear', as Jamaicans say. You were safe. I hadn't stopped to consider that the BBC was still a microcosm of British society, and that there were people inside this liberal institution who would continue to view me, a black man, with suspicion. Somewhere along the line in my adult life I was bound to have had to answer this charge. You are a black man; eventually someone is going to label you 'aggressive'. When your accuser is a white woman, you will be doubly indicted. There is the actuality of the contemporary allegation itself to contend with, but also the historical one; for black men over centuries have been charged with menacing or interfering with white women. I should have seen it coming.

Looking back now, the route to my investigation could be traced to the arrival of the new manager. Prior to that, we'd worked in small groups of four or five, almost hermetically sealed in book-lined offices, in a discrete and civilised environment. The new manager came in with fresh ideas to knock down internal walls to create a huge, open-plan space. Privately my colleagues were outraged, but at a meeting to discuss the plans, nobody demurred. When it was my turn to speak, I said I didn't like open-plan offices because it made me think of plantation life, with the overseer in the big house looking out over the slaves toiling in the cotton fields. Everybody, apart from the manager, laughed.

After the meeting the manager chased after me, cornered and then corralled me into a small workshop. When the door was closed, there was no room even to turn around. We were only inches apart. I could feel her warm breath on my face as she struggled to contain her rage.

'How dare you accuse me of wanting to be a slave owner!' she screamed.

Recounting the episode to my uncle later that evening, he berated me for being so foolish. What if, my uncle wanted to know, the manager later claimed that, in that tiny workshop, I'd touched her?

'Don't be daft. This is the BBC, not—'

'Not what?' Uncle Viv interrupted. 'Not an Antebellum plantation?'

During the following week, it became clear that an old, familiar trope was being played out; the lustful and aggressive black man threatening the intimidated white woman, a fragrant damsel in distress (in danger of being molested), in need of a chivalric saviour.

*

The hearing rolled on and on interminably. All along, my blackness coloured the perception of me; any sense of my character disappeared and dominant assumptions about the black man (I was representative of the race) were reasserted. But over the months of interrogation, it became increasingly clear that I was not being scrutinised for my aggression; rather, I was on trial for not fitting in, for having duped them. I was not the pliant soul they had believed me to be when I had accepted the invitation to join the corporation; I was not one of them.

It was as if I were a Trojan Horse, let through the gates of Bush House into the sacred space of the institution. I'd only fully revealed myself once I was safely inside and was now bent on burning down the master's house. The managers had realised, too late, their mistake. The retrograde invitation to a disciplinary hearing was a manifestation of that.

Six months after the investigation began, I was summoned to The Man's office to hear the verdict. As I took a seat, he barely looked up. His eyes were fixed on the sheet of paper with the verdict. He slowly read out the full details of the original and expanded terms of the enquiry. Finally he lifted his head, took off his glasses and sighed. 'The charge against you is not proven.'

This essay will form part of the author's forthcoming memoir.

The Cuban Missile Crisis

Jethro Soutar

'Have you ever been in a fistfight?'

Not your usual first question in a job interview, but then the preliminary round of most job interviews is not the Lüschercolour test.

I didn't know that's what it was at the time. I remember sitting there staring at the eight coloured cards – blue, yellow, red, green, purple, brown, grey, black – and wondering what on Earth I was supposed to do. I'd been told to 'put them in order'.

'What sort of order?' I asked.

'Whatever order feels right,' said the man from Recruitment.

'You mean like a rainbow?'

'If that's how you want to do it.'

This was London in the 2000s. I'd been living abroad, had just moved back to the UK and needed a job. After applying to several, this was the only reply I'd got. It was a researcher position at a company operating in the legal sector, starting salary £18,000. There'd been no mention of a good eye for colour in the job description.

A few minutes passed. Aware that I ought to show some initiative, I took a deep breath and rearranged the cards into a sort of progressive order, more of a paint chart than a rainbow. The man from Recruitment wrote my selection down and left the room.

I'd just taken Max Lüscher's personality test. A Swiss psychotherapist, he developed the test in the late 1940s based on the premise that colour preferences are guided by the unconscious and reveal deep personality traits. Blue, yellow, red and green are considered the 'basic' colours, and placing them early in the sequence indicates a well-balanced individual.

Purple, brown, grey and black are the 'auxiliary' colours, and favouring them implies a negative attitude to life.

I can't remember what order I chose, but it was evidently sufficient to pass myself off as stable and positive; when the Recruitment man came back, he told me to go upstairs and meet the boss.

The boss was a man in his sixties who I'll call CM. He owned the company and it bore his name; indeed, it still does, though it's under new management. His office was a small study with a large desk and leather-bound books crammed on shelves. I went in and sat down and he pretended not to notice me. Two or three minutes went by, and I wondered if I should say something, whether this might not be another test of initiative. But it was a bit late for that; I'd set out my stall as polite and patient, and it was probably best to stick to it.

After perhaps ten minutes, he feigned sudden awareness of my presence. He fumbled about for a piece of paper, presumably my CV, and overacted the reading of it, making pained and astonished facial expressions. Then he asked: 'Have you ever been in a fistfight?'

Actually, that wasn't the question he asked me. I heard about that from someone else later. My question was tame in comparison: 'Why is there so little realism in Latin American literature?'

This might make some sense as a question to ask me now; I'm a literary translator and have translated novels from Brazil and Argentina. But I hadn't done anything like that at the time. My CV would have mentioned that I'd written about South American football and cinema and this, presumably, was enough of a cue.

I was surprised by the question, but it also put me at ease. The strangeness of the day began to make sense; he was trying to unsettle me to see how I'd react. Fine. I'd been to university, I knew the game. I told him that, actually, there was plenty of realism in Latin American literature, it was just that magic realism had become popular internationally. We had a bit of back and forth about it. I defended my argument and got the job.

At the end of my first week, I went to the pub with my new colleagues. 'So what random question did the old bugger ask you?' someone said. It turned out that all candidates were treated to pretty much the same routine. We went around the table comparing opening gambits:

'Do you play a musical instrument?'

'Have you ever swallowed a spider?'

'Alfred Hitchcock was a terrible hack, wasn't he?'

'Can you explain the Israel–Palestine conflict to me?'

'Do you believe in sex before marriage?'

'Spanish is a very limited language, isn't it?'

'Would you say twenty-seven is young or old?'

'Have you ever been in a fistfight?'

A French colleague was asked, 'Have you ever robbed a bank?', which sounds amusing and, indeed, he laughs about it now. But at the time, as a young man attending a first job interview in a foreign country in a different language, he'd found it so disconcerting that he'd rung his mum afterwards to tell her he was moving back to France. He couldn't believe it when he got the job.

Having no cultural reference point could also be an advantage. A Lithuanian colleague was asked, 'Do you have a boyfriend?' This being her first job interview in the UK, she assumed it was standard procedure, rather than intrusive and inappropriate, and answered matter-of-factly; next question.

How you respond to strange questions also depends on your idea of 'strange'. When I asked another friend about her interview, she said, 'Oh, mine wasn't weird at all, we just discussed trends in postmodernist art theory.'

Not everyone was asked a question. I heard of someone who was told to do a dance; another was led around a nearby gallery; another was taken for a walk. The office was near Smithfield Market, an old area of London full of cut-throughs and alleyways, and midway through the walk – actually, mid-conversation – CM disappeared. My future workmate stood around for a while, then went home. He, too, was astonished to get the job.

A Brazilian friend swears she was hired only because she mentioned in passing that she'd once lived on a canal barge; the interview had been a disaster up until then. And a Cuban friend has no doubt that he got the job because he was Cuban; the interview went on for over an hour and consisted entirely of questions about life in Cuba. He wasn't even asked to do the written English test usually required of non-native speakers.

CM's love of Cuba was well-known among staff. One colleague shared this fact with a friend who was coming in for an interview. The friend had been to Cuba earlier in the year.

'I understand you like Cuba,' he had said, cracking under the strain of the silent treatment. 'I was there recently.'

CM looked up from whatever he was pretending to do and said, 'Tell me about the Cuban Missile Crisis.'

'Well, oh...' the friend stuttered. 'It was only a quick visit, I didn't pick up much of the history.'

'You don't know anything about the Cuban Missile Crisis?'

'Not as such ... It was just a holiday, really.'

'Get out.'

'I'm sorry?'

'Get out. The interview's over.'

'But...'

'If you went somewhere and showed so little interest in it that you can't tell me the first thing about its history, then we've no need for you here. Goodbye.'

Harsh, certainly. But unfair? Most of us could see a twisted kind of logic to what happened. There was even a general sense of bemused admiration for the recruitment process among staff. Of course there was; we'd all passed the test, so it was nice to think it was uniquely demanding, that only mavericks need apply. Plus, it did seem to work. For an office of over a hundred people, there were very few slackers or egos, and there was also a genuine sense of community — the best I've ever known in a workplace. I made several friends for life there. Could this really have been because of a quirky interview and a New Age personality test?

The rumour in the office was that you got to the second stage of the interview provided that you didn't pick black first in the colour test; black is deemed to be the worst of the 'auxiliary' colours, representing negation and nothingness. But there seemed to be more to the company's use of the test than that. A Colombian colleague spoke of going upstairs to find CM practically salivating over his colour score: 'Very good colours — very, very good colours!' He got the job and was promoted as soon as an opening came up.

I also heard of a starter who was introduced to her team as being 'an exceptionally sexual person' according to the colour test. Besides being offensive and outrageous, the episode is illustrative of a broader truth.

The eccentric interview process was not ultimately indicative of an environment where left-field thinking thrived, but one where staff were in thrall to the erratic whims of the boss. His management style was based on power games, bullying and sleazy sexism, as his interviewing technique forewarned. It's abusive for a man in his sixties to ask a girl in her twenties to talk about sex before marriage when it's in his gift to offer her a job. He told another friend she reminded him of a Picasso painting.

'Hopefully not from his Cubist period,' she'd replied.

'No,' said CM. 'I was thinking of one of his nudes.'

In other words, the wackiness was just a gloss for a business culture that is now, thankfully, being challenged and cancelled.

Why didn't we challenge and cancel it ourselves? Because they were different times? Because we couldn't be bothered? Because we were too desperate for a job? It was a little of all of these things which, if nothing else, helps to explain the office camaraderie. For most people the job was not a career choice, but a means to an end while we sought fortunes in more creative fields or experienced life in London; and this, rather than the mumbo-jumbo of personality tests, brought like-minded people together.

Besides, the majority of positions required fluency in English and one other language. People speak two languages for all sorts of reasons, all of them interesting, and this made for a vibrant and diverse workplace — diverse, at least in terms of nationality; it was pretty white for London. Was this another product of the pseudo-science? Did black candidates not associate black with negation and nothingness?

As for my Colombian friend, never mind his favourite colour, he was good at the job and eminently qualified for it; no wonder he got promoted. But promotion meant moving up the pyramid and coming into closer contact with the boss. One Monday morning he was summoned to CM's office.

'It's about the new guy,' CM said. 'We've made a terrible mistake.'

CM had interviewed a young Brazilian man the previous week and my Colombian friend had called him on the Friday to tell him he'd got the job.

'What do you mean "a mistake"?'

'His father's a baker!'

'Right. And... ?'

'A baker's son! How could I be so stupid? I haven't been able to sleep all weekend.'

'I'm not sure I—'

'You'll have to call him back,' said CM. 'Tell him he's not quite right for us after all.'

Whether this was simple class prejudice or something more hocus-pocus we'll never know. CM rushed off, meeting over, leaving my friend to traipse back upstairs and make the fateful phone call. He did it, then sat at his desk and thought about the job and the company and the man he worked for. He handed in his notice the next week.

Exactly as I Am

Kerry Hudson

This middle place, a hinterland neither here nor there, is somewhere I am familiar with. It is often how I have described my feelings about class and my position in society. Floating between two identities, but claimed by neither. Rootless and placeless.

Of course, I have written widely about background, class and poverty. I wrote a whole book about returning to the working-class communities I grew up in. In 2019 I travelled the length and breadth of the country and spoke to over 100 audiences, from the London Palladium to University of St Andrews, about class and poverty. I talked on radio and TV. I wrote articles and essays. Each time I approached these topics from a singular, seemingly inarguable standpoint: this was my life growing up working class, this is the impact it had on me as an adult, this is what we might be able to do to lessen the damage of poverty. One of many things I learned during this time is that people are very nervous about the filthy 'C' word. (That's *class*, by the way; I can't imagine what you were you thinking of.)

I also learned that my inarguable standpoint of self-identification and lived experience seemed, well, arguable to many. How, I was asked, could I still call myself working class if I was sitting on a stage or writing in a newspaper? Wasn't my childhood simply chaotic and deprived? Didn't I grow up with a parent who was struggling, while living in care homes and B&Bs? That's not working class, they told me, that's individual dysfunction. The ones who didn't understand how little writers make asked if I wasn't too financially comfortable now to call myself working class. Others felt that, even if I did earn the same as the manager of a small shop, my cultural capital made me undeserving.

Still others wished me to bestow upon them, somehow, a seal of approval, or to validate them: a crib sheet for 'working classness'. *My parents were comfortable,* they said, <insert 'middle-class' profession here>, *but brought me up with working-class principles; am I working class? Who gets to decide if I'm working class or not?* (Spoiler: not me.) *If you make your living doing something as 'luxurious' or 'self-indulgent' as art* (please note my added sarcasm here), *can you be working class? Is it insulting to be called working class? Is it virtue signalling to make the claim? Does the working class even exist anymore?*

As class-straitjacketed as Britain is, it seems it is not as binary as many might hope. Ultimately, these 'rules' have always been variable, and have become ever more so as our society, workforce and access to income, welfare, education and social mobility morph with each decade and change in government policy.

I admit I have exploited these ambiguities in defining myself in the past — when given very little option if I was to move through worlds that were not my own, say; or when I had to learn the language and customs quickly or be banished. I did it at university, carving away my sharp council-estate edges (and a lot of my personality) to try to fit in with the public school Mirandas. I did it again at twenty-three, starting out in a job with an NGO at the top of a shiny skyscraper by the Thames, not knowing how to add an email attachment but knowing well enough that I should never mention where I came from, the benefits queues or care homes. I did it at thirty-two, at impressive parties, standing in gilded rooms drinking white wine, smiling sweetly while people who owned two houses asked me archly, *where is that accent from?* and stayed silent while they tried to sort me into a hierarchy they could feel comfortable with. I have done it even just shy of forty, a best-selling and prize-winning author, listening to a radio producer saying that, despite my upbringing, I must 'read and write well enough, at least.'

I have travelled everywhere within this hinterland, and still felt neither here nor there. But what has saved me, what has allowed me to navigate a society that desperately wanted to categorise and catalogue me, denying me the agency to do so myself, is that I have identified as working class my whole life. Not always for others' benefit, but within myself, in my bones and marrow. I learned that it's not a *place*, after all; it's a foundation, something solid upon which to stand.

I have always felt part of the rich culture of people who keep society turning, who keep living tenaciously, even though the lives of better-off folk are stacked on their shoulders. When I meet someone who also grew up on a council estate – even knowing that not all council estates, not all upbringings, are created equal – I feel a sense of kinship. Do you know what it's like to wait hungrily for the benefits book to be cashed or for payday to come around? Was it not simply assumed that you'd learn to drive, or go to university, or eventually have a mortgage? Then yes, you're part of my tribe — large and diverse though it is.

If you are like me, you've also experienced meeting someone and feeling that shared understanding of background, culture and challenges faced daily. It's both comforting and empowering to connect with someone who simply *recognises* you, though you've never met before.

No, it's not that I just grew up 'poor' which, after all, focuses only on economics when, in fact, inequality in our society, where we find ourselves in the hierarchy, affects everything: life expectancy, educational attainment, likelihood of mental illness.

Last year, in the face of so many questions from audiences, I began to ask myself: in whose interests is it to dismantle the working class by protesting that it doesn't exist anymore? Who benefits from the erasure and silencing of the many of us who would publicly call ourselves working-class teachers, artists, bin-men, bankers, social workers, cashiers, writers, nurses and solicitors?

Certainly, it is not the people who seek to give greater voice to those besieged, in a country where every government policy seems designed to accelerate the decline of poorer communities.

It's not those who understand that being working class doesn't just mean to be poor, or on the dole, or struggling with a zero-hours contract, but that it is a psychology and a legacy, both good and hard, all of its own.

I no longer apologise for the fact that I defy checklists of stereotypes. In fact, I no longer entertain this line of questioning at all, which is designed to make the other person feel more secure by knocking me from solid ground. No one gets to define me, even if they think they're entitled to — and by the way, why would they think that in the first place? I came to understand why, for many, it is difficult to accept that the working class contains multitudes. Because in that solidarity there lies real power.

So, I will exist in this in-between place forever. But I get to choose where I focus my work, where I find my foundations. This middle place is *exactly* where I'm meant to be. These margins are where our voices are expected to be quiet, where we're meant to become small, so that we might squeeze into one permitted space or another. But I am not small and I am not quiet, and I know I am where I need to be and right, exactly as I am.

The Boy with No Race?

Johny Pitts

In 2019, my book *Afropean: Notes from Black Europe* was published by Penguin. Though it was broadly well-received, a few disgruntled commentators aired grievances, as though I was some new hipster who had burst out of nowhere and claimed all the glory for the hard work they'd secretly been doing behind the scenes for years (so secret, in fact, that it was usually people I'd never heard of, who hadn't actually been very active). 'If someone has anointed a black intellectual' wrote Henry Louis Gates Jnr, 'be assured that others are busily constructing his tumbril.'

I was prepared for this, because I'd been guilty of unwarranted misgivings about other, younger writers being published when I wasn't. Communities that don't get their fair share of the spotlight can go two ways when appraising their own: supreme pride or vengeful resentment. And with good reason — there is modicum of truth in the idea that there is only enough space for a few key black success stories in a white media landscape. Every time another black writer gets published, it can feel as though you've been robbed of your portion of an already finite availability of resources.

My journey to an audience for *Afropean*, however, was hard won, taking the best part of fifteen years and leaving me in debt, because I'd had to self-finance the bulk of my travel and research before anyone would take a chance on me. I'd floated different versions of the idea around to officialdom: a late-night music show, for instance, playing French hip-hop, German reggae, Swedish soul (and so on) when I had a short stint at BBC Radio 1xtra. (I wanted to play Youssou N'Dour and Stromae; they wanted me to talk about what Beyoncé wore to the Grammys.) I pitched the idea of a trip around Europe meeting with black communities to one publisher, who told me 'It's already been done' — referring to Caryl Phillips's *The European Tribe*, written around the time I was born. The publisher suggested Blackness in Europe was monolithic, that it had not shifted after three decades in which the geopolitical structure of the continent had been radically transformed. I wrote a treatment for a documentary and offered it to various channels, who all told me it was 'too niche' — a common refrain that usually meant 'too black'.

This was often stated in that oblivious way white, middle-class men who don't consider themselves capable of racism say *Mate, why are you going on about being black? You're British, race doesn't matter.* By contrast, a producer told a friend of mine, after a screen test to present a TV show, that he'd given a great audition but that, unfortunately, they 'already had a black presenter'. Similarly, when I was whittled down to the final two to co-present *Blue Peter* with Ayo Akinwolere, one of my best friends since my teenage years, I knocked the screen test out of the park; but they chose a white presenter with much less experience (who was sacked little over a year later because of his ineptness), and told me I was 'too similar' to Ayo. I am working class, from Sheffield; Ayo is an upper middle-class Nigerian; clearly, there was only enough space for any one black person at a time. *So being black doesn't make a difference anymore? I'm British, race doesn't matter?*

The closest I came to getting anything like *Afropean* off the ground was when a production company expressed interest. After an initial period of excitement, they sent back a bastardised treatment of my idea with a new title: *The Boy with No Race: A Search for Belonging.* Telling the story of black Europeans wasn't enough; the documentary had to have a narrative arc, be transfigured into a patronising 'journey of discovery' for white viewers to understand, so that it wasn't 'too niche'. I have sold out many times in the media industry to pay the bills, but thankfully this wasn't one of those occasions.

I was not a 'boy' with no race. I was a black creative with no *place*, kept at bay by a media industry and a country with 'no race'; which is to say that Britain in the Noughties believed itself to be 'post-racial'. During that time, I came up against an endless number of glass ceilings, only to bump my head and fall back into reductive or redundant bit parts; I was never offered a contract lasting longer than six months, and even when I'd held certain roles for years, they were kept on precarious rolling contracts, which don't allow you to plan for anything. Worse, back then even *I* didn't really believe that the walls I kept coming up against were connected to racism. It was inconceivable to me that my ideas might not have been taken seriously because systemic racism was at work. Looking back, even if this notion ever did cross my mind, I probably sensed it would have been unhelpful to admit it. Creative industries are about relationships — and how could you ever prove such a thing?

In the course of bringing a project to light, everybody – regardless of race – will endure setbacks, and sometimes for good reason. I was too young, at the age of twenty, to grapple with some of the questions I wanted to explore about black European identity. I needed to hone my craft, put in my hours, serve my apprenticeship; *Afropean* found its final form when it needed to. Yet during the course of my career, I'd seen others breeze through doors I had to fight to enter; they were allowed to fail and learn on the job, while I had to do things *outside* the job, in a constant state of precarity.

Everything that went into my book was forged during self-funded hours outside the random array of remunerated work to keep myself afloat. As the late cultural theorist Mark Fisher wrote of neoliberal Britain in the twenty-first century: 'If you want to engage in a twenty-year long research project funded by the state, you will have to kill someone.' This is particularly true if you have brown skin. I knew I wasn't cut out for prison, so the killing had to be figurative ... and the person who needed to be 'killed' was 'post-racial' me.

You see, I'm from a generation of Eighties babies — technically 'millennial', but old enough to remember the twentieth century and become nostalgic about the Nineties and Noughties as the era of fusion and multiculturalism, erring towards the 'post-racial': a bold, forward-looking Britain with Blair at the helm. But, as Svetlana Boym wrote in her opus *The Future of Nostalgia*:

> Nostalgia (from *nostos* – return home, and *algia* – longing) is a longing for a home that no longer exists or *has never existed*. Nostalgia is a sentiment of loss and displacement, but it is also a romance with one's own fantasy. Nostalgic love can only survive in a long-distance relationship. A cinematic image of nostalgia is a double exposure, or a superimposition of two images — of home and abroad, past and present, dream and everyday life. The moment we try to force it into a single image, it breaks the frame or burns the surface. [Emphasis mine.]

Only in the writing of this piece have I recognised acutely just how awful the decade in which my generation came of age – the 2000s – actually was in terms of representation. The obliviousness in Britain back then seems hard to believe now. Books such as *The Idler Book of Crap Towns* by writers educated at Oxbridge were being published before they could envision that the residents of a vast majority of those towns would vote to leave Europe to spite exactly the type of dickheads capable of conceiving such a book. Words like *chav* were bandied around. Black culture was broadly mocked by the heroin-chic indie generation, which gave us ironic posh-boy guitar covers of gangsta rap anthems; hip-hop was culturally appropriated across the board, to the point where the whole *raison d'être* of YouTube rap battles seemed to be for educated white kids pretending to be street to 'own' a black kid actually *from* the street, with rhythmical insults. It was an era in which Noel Gallagher tried to prevent Jay-Z from playing at Glastonbury, but not Kylie Minogue or Fatboy Slim. Terms such as 'ghetto-fabulous' were being used, and there were trendy venues with names like 'Favela Chic'. To express frustration at all this was to be branded a fringe radical obsessed with 'playing the race card', because it was a period in which the notion of political blackness had waned, swallowed up by the cultural industries — something I wrote about in *Afropean*:

> In an excellent 2004 conversation between Kodwo Eshun and John Akomfrah about the Black Audio Film Collective, which I cherish as being one of the most inspirational and foremost examples of black British collective excellence, Eshun paraphrases the art critic Kobena Mercer: '[We now live in] an era of multicultural normalization, in which diversity is increasingly administered as a social and cultural norm in postmodernity'. Mercer went on to say that contemporary artists no longer feel responsible for constructing Afrodiasporic presence as an object of knowledge in the marketplace of multicultural commodity fetishism.

This chimes with something French anthropologist and essayist Marc Augé wrote:

> Before they are even formulated, calls for pluralism, for diversity, for recasting, for the redefinition of criteria, for openness to other cultures, are absorbed, proclaimed, trivialised and staged by the system, meaning in concrete terms by the media, the fixed and moving image, the political and other authorities. The difficulty facing art, in the broadest sense of the word, has always been to distance itself from a society that it has to embody, nonetheless, if it wants to be understood … it has to be expressive and reflexive if it wants to show us anything we do not see daily on TV or in the supermarket.

In essence, the very thing that so successfully intellectualised a whole generation was the thing that generation began *rejecting* in order to move forward.

As we return to political blackness, there is already a lot of kickback. Thomas Chatterton Williams (a writer I admire for his elegant prose and intellectual integrity, but with whom I frequently disagree) is keen to bring back the project of moving beyond race. He was one of the original group who penned the infamous 'cancel culture' letter for *Harper's*, lamenting the trend towards hard-line activism that all too eagerly tears people and structures down. Thomas is a self-described 'woke-sceptic', and his book *Unlearning Race* proposes a future in which his blonde, blue-eyed daughter might, when she's older, find race an arbitrary construct as she sips wine with her multicultural, post-racial group of friends. The vision he presents is very attractive, but whereas its outcome feels sensible and sane, the proposal of how we might arrive at such a post-racial place is missing. I identify with Thomas, who is only a couple of years older than me, because I feel that people in their early twenties sometimes do confuse rudeness for revolution, and the way icons of a previous generation are destroyed over something as little as an off-key comment on social media doesn't resonate with me. However, as much as I identify with youth culture of the Nineties and Noughties, and the more laid-back cultural atmosphere I perceive in memories of that time, I would not want to go back. *Afropean*, a work that is perhaps gentler and more charitable across cultures than other books released recently, would probably not have survived a world in such denial as it was a decade ago.

People might look at the 2010s negatively but it was, at least, a time in which a great reckoning came to pass, when chickens came home to roost and issues never tackled in polite company were brought out into the light, producing a landscape now 'waking' up to its racism. I would even argue that Thomas's own work would not have found an audience had it not been for the very 'woke' commentators he criticises so vehemently; for they are the ones with the kind of completely unapologetic stance needed to open up a space for intelligent black writing, ready to tear down prevailing systems in which they aren't as invested.

In many ways, my generation of Eighties babies find ourselves standing on the shoulders of people ten years younger than us, as much as those of our elders. For it is they who have seized upon some of the innovations of capitalism in creative and often provocative ways, using technologies originally geared against them to generate a following and sustain their work. Despite the chaos of the last decade, with all the division and misinformation, it is now possible – and this is crucial and unprecedented – to circumnavigate the middle (-class white) man, who would turn *Afropean* into *The Boy with No Race*, if he even gave it a chance at all. I was published after self-funding my trip around Europe, and though I'd like to think it was on the strength of my work, the real reason I got a book deal is, I believe, because I had built my own online platform, afropean. com, which in turn attracted a dedicated following over the years outside of any official spaces. The same holds true of people like Reni Eddo-Lodge, another working-class writer whose widely successful *Why I'm No Longer Talking to White People About Race* emerged from a blog post, and George the Poet, whose *Have You Heard George's Podcast* was produced and platformed online independently before being snapped up by the BBC. When floodgates open, it's true that quality doesn't always match quantity, but who cares? People are being published, learning what it's like to work with an editor, how to give radio interviews, deal with criticism; they are giving themselves the experiences and opportunities that were once denied by standard-bearers in an industry standoffish to those outside the Oxbridge circuit.

The only time I've been able to achieve a post-racial state of mind is when I'm buffered by the comfort of a scene in which independent, empowered political blackness looms large. The health of this dialectic between individual goals and community empowerment is absolutely essential if this encouraging moment of black creativity is to continue into the 2020s and beyond.

Vigilantes That Kill

Fergal Harte

Mon, 28 Sept, 12:43
(14 days ago)

Francis Castiglione <f.castle@gmail.com>

To Edward

I ain't a poet, so don't expect this shit to rhyme.
  1 Attachment: war_journal.PDF

03/09

New York City. Rain. Preferable to the desert. It was simpler over there. Back home it's more complicated. Not as complicated as our boys and girls in Spandex would have you believe, but more recon is required before you can shoot. Saw kid arrested while on run. Kid must've been fifteen or sixteen. Junior would've been about that age now. Kept running. Wanted to get inside. About to go in when cop car passed. Kid inside. Officer headed towards docks, not precinct. Had to follow. Hate it when cops feel need to become the monster. Unnecessary. My purpose, not theirs. Grabbed bag by door. Followed on foot.

Car stopped by warehouse. Two men by door. Kid escorted inside by cop. Climbed shipping containers far enough away not to be seen. Used drone. Idiots had left roof window open. Slipped drone in. Kid was in cage with a dozen others. Guards shouted at them. SHUT UP. SCUM. I WILL KILL YOU. Threats not empty. Spotted guards dumping bodies into oil barrels. Liquid inside barrels dissolved bodies. Good method. Used it myself many times. Cop from earlier was only one in uniform. Found out later the rest were off-duty or retired. Eight guards. Ten with two at door. All armed. Retrieved drone. Checked gun. Colt 1911. Classic. Seven rounds per mag. Two mags. Sufficient.

'Excuse me, sir. You <u>can't</u> be here. Private property.'

Bent down to catch breath.

'One second, just passing through.'

One came closer.

'Sir, you really can't—'

Drew gun. Dropped the big ones. Rain helped muffle sound, only one came out.

'What the hell is going on?'

Dropped him too. They all heard that. Went round side. Used grapple hook to get up to open window. Three were stacked up by main door. Two hid behind desk. One behind the oil barrel he had been stuffing bodies into seconds earlier. The cop tried the back door. It was locked.

I didn't waste time. Four shots. Four down. Reloaded. Five shots. Rest down. The cop was slippery. Went inside, checked bodies for cage key. All had matching tattoos. Made pretty clear they were all fans of old Adolf's work. Found key. Opened cage. Called Heroes for Hire. Made way home.

Good run.

Edward Cruise <ted.cruise@vtknet.com>

To Francis

Hi Frank,

Thank you so much for your submission! As you know, all of us over at Vigilantes That Kill are massive fans of your work so it was a real honour to receive a piece from you — so, again, thank you!

Unfortunately, in its current form, your piece is not quite right for us. We are simply not sure that it would be appropriate for our readers.

You see, we have conducted numerous surveys of our subscribers over the years and have discovered that 78% of our most loyal readers are employed by the various regional and federal law enforcement agencies of our great nation. Because of this, we feel that a piece which compares you and them (they really look up to you!) to 'monsters' might not send the right message. An excerpt featuring some of the less desirable elements of our brave police force has similar issues, especially in the current political climate (everyone has some sort of racial bias anyway, am I right?).

As such, we would greatly appreciate it if you submitted a different excerpt from your *War Journal* (what an awesome title, by the way), one that features bad guys who are, you know, actually bad — maybe some drug dealers or pimps, for example. I am sure you have put down many of them over the years!

We look forward to reading your next submission.

Best wishes,

Ted Cruise
Deputy Editor, Vigilantes That Kill

VTK
Supporting true American heroes.
Vigilantes That Kill is a monthly, independently run publication. For any queries or submissions, please contact a member of staff via our website.

Sun, 4 Oct, 23:56
(8 days ago)

Edward Cruise <ted.cruise@vtknet.com>

To Francis

Hi Frank,

We are mere minutes away from printing our next issue. Do you have that second submission for us? Because we need it. Like yesterday.

Best wishes,

Ted Cruise
Deputy Editor, Vigilantes That Kill

VTK
Supporting true American heroes.
Vigilantes That Kill is a monthly, independently run publication. For any queries or submissions, please contact a member of staff via our website.

V travel

'the Tube is billowing with an ache'

Excerpt: 'Prologue' from *Abolition*

Gabriel Gbadamosi

CAST of *ABOLITION*:
In Order of Appearance

The SURGEON, Mr Jones
The PURSER, Tom
The CAPTAIN, John Knox
The BOSUN, Mr Palmer
A SLAVE
The CABIN-BOY, part of the CREW
John TARLETON, a Liverpool Merchant
JAKE, Knox's Slave
The NEGER SHANTYMAN, part of the SHANTY CHORUS
William FOX, Quaker
William WILBERFORCE, MP (for Hull)
CROWD Scenes, the MOB
MAN, at the Cock-Fight
JENNY, Tarleton's Daughter
FIDDLER, part of the Press-GANG
William PITT, the Younger, Prime Minister
Archibald BALZIEL, a Bristol Captain

PROLOGUE

The Dead List

Cabin of the Blackamoor Jenny. *TOM writes in the ship's book. The SURGEON dictates, cleaning and gathering his bloody tools into a bag.*

SURGEON: … Nicholas, before the mast, with an Intermittent Fever.

Mr Young, apprentice Sail-maker, with a Bilious Fever.

The Armourer — died.

The Cook — died.

The Carpenter, with a Head-Ache, but refused Medicine — died.

Jack Reynolds — died.

Jack Strahan, with a Diarrhoea.

Harry, with the bloody Flux.

The boy Peter — died.

The SURGEON stops, gazing in air, as if trying to remember someone. TOM waits a moment.

TOM: Should we not record the Cause of Death in all Cases?

SURGEON: By all means, Purser. Your Guess is as good as mine.

TOM: Does that complete the Dead List?

The SURGEON gestures for him to continue writing.

SURGEON: To date. 5th March, 1792. Arrived at our Moorings at the Mouth of the Niger with 47 crew. In three Weeks of our Stay on the Coast, 11 sewn in their Hammocks and committed. And a further 7 took ill with Exhaustion and Fever. The Rump of our Crew-Men stalked by the Yellow Jack … A murderous Fellow, somewhat shadowy in Appearance; his Attack made even more terrible by the ivory-yellowness of his Skin and Teeth, and the suddenness of Death on his Approach … Officers of the After-Guard being, of course, exempt.

117

TOM has stopped writing. He crosses out, and turns the book towards the SURGEON.

TOM: Sign here.

The SURGEON takes the pen and signs. The CAPTAIN enters.

SURGEON: … Mr Jones, Surgeon …

CAPTAIN: What's this?

TOM: Drawing up the Dead List, Sir.

CAPTAIN: Waste Work! The Cargo's not complete. I want my Men up and doing.

SURGEON: The Dead?

CAPTAIN: Sarcasm, Surgeon? Your Knife were better honed in finding Cures.

SURGEON: The best Cure's to be away on open Sea. The Crew need Air, and Food, and Rest; to be better provisioned and out of the way of the Coast. This is hopeless.

CAPTAIN: No Work, no Food. We go nowhere without a full Haul.

SURGEON: You can't Starve sick men.

CAPTAIN: You argue with me?

SURGEON: Without a Crew, Captain, we're stuck.

The CAPTAIN strikes down the SURGEON, wounding him in the head. TOM, in shock, instinctively bends to him.

CAPTAIN: Leave him! Die, and be damned!

TOM hesitates, then disobeys. He helps the SURGEON back onto a chair. The SURGEON takes a swab from his bag and holds it to the wound. He looks at the CAPTAIN.

SURGEON: Not dead, Capt. Knox, Sir … You may chance to need me yet.

TOM: *(To the CAPTAIN)* Sir, with Sickness, depletion of our Stores, no Slaves to buy at the Factories and none being brought down to them, we cannot wait much longer. It's my Duty as Purser to tell you so. We must make a Decision: Stay or Go. What will you do?

CAPTAIN: What more Slaves do we need to make us profitable?

TOM: Another 60. We have 286, or thereabouts. With no further Losses we could break even. Should Sickness begin to rot our Cargo at the same Rate as the Crew, it would be a losing Voyage. For you, and my Uncle.

CAPTAIN: Show me the Account. *(To the SURGEON)* Go examine the Negroes aboard, what State they're in. Report how many can make the Crossing. I'll decide what's needed.

The CAPTAIN turns to inspect the ship's accounts. The SURGEON throws down his swab and rises shakily, still bleeding from the head.

TOM: Are you up to it?

SURGEON: I have my Doubts.

The SURGEON takes up his bag and looks at TOM.

> Do you?

TOM: I doubt you were made for this Trade. I cannot afford to doubt myself.

SURGEON: The Slaves are waiting.

The CAPTAIN turns.

CAPTAIN: Keep your Head, Mr Jones. And I may give you the Chance to mend it.

The SURGEON goes. TOM sits back with the ship's accounts. The CAPTAIN paces.

TOM: As of now it's clear, the *Jenny* must make a losing Voyage.

The CAPTAIN kicks over a chair.

> Our Hands are bound by the Factories: their Prices, Slaves scarce. We cannot trade freely in anything with the Natives. In my Opinion, she must always make a losing Voyage.

CAPTAIN: As for your Opinion, Purser, give me Facts!

TOM: On current Prices, a Short-Fall of above 100 Pound Sterling.

The CAPTAIN paces in thought. TOM closes the book.

> Bound to be a losing Voyage.

CAPTAIN: Bound? Bound where? Bound to a Profit for any further Command! Bound to nothing! Open the Book! I'll bind her 'fore she leaks my Profit!

TOM opens the book.

Aye, Bound, with one Bound for Home, and home on Profit! What Wages?

TOM looks.

TOM: 400 in Spanish dollars; 400 in Pound Sterling on our Return to Liverpool.

The CAPTAIN paces.

CAPTAIN: Subtract for Deaths.

TOM: We pay Wages for the Dead.

CAPTAIN: Then we plank the Sick down on the West India Wharfs with half their Pay. How lightens that the Standing of our Profit?

TOM: The Crew's contracted for a Return Voyage.

CAPTAIN: Profit's what we carry Home — and no Man comes on Freight!

TOM: Their contract is for Half – the better Half, in Sterling – on our Return. We can't plank down half-Dead. Our Crew's depleted as it is.

CAPTAIN: There's ten strong Men for every One that's Gone, to take up Slack and haul a Passage home!

TOM closes the book.

TOM: The Balance of their Lives thrown in for Profit?

Banging and shouts from offstage; they turn to the sound.

BOSUN (*off*):   They strike, damn you! Close it, shut the Hatch!

TOM and the CAPTAIN pass from the cabin to the deck. They meet the BOSUN dragging a SLAVE, handcuffed and thumb-screwed in praying position, both legs shackled and stumbling. The BOSUN pulls on the chain attached to a collar about the neck. There is a grille over the head, open at the mouth, making the SLAVE faceless.

TOM: (*To the BOSUN*) What's here?

CAPTAIN: Learn by Example, what is Customary to do. Stand back.

BOSUN: They won't eat.

The BOSUN stands behind, forcing back the head, and inserts a 'speculum oris' into the SLAVE's mouth (a vice with forward blade and backward hooks).

            The Thumb-Screw's to take out the Stubbornness. This opens his Mouth. Stand back. (*Forces it open*) Grub's up. Our Promise: we won't eat you.

The SURGEON enters, drenched in sweat, his head still bloody and his shoes off. The soles of his feet leave imprints of blood across the deck. He approaches and pulls open an eye of the SLAVE, lifts and drops the jaw, and examines the rusted chain around the neck, finding a chafed wound.

SURGEON: This isn't Hunger. It's Locked-Jaw.

TOM sees the SURGEON's feet and looks at the trail of blood across the deck.

TOM: Where are your shoes?

SURGEON: It's Impossible to go amongst them with my Shoes on — they lie so close together I should have hurt them if I did. I have the Mark upon my Feet of Skin and Blood, of Effluence, the Putrefaction of their lying in the 'Tween-Decks.

CAPTAIN: What Condition are they in? Can they make the Crossing?

SURGEON: Am I to re-create Man from Slime? I cannot do it!

A Silence. The CABIN-BOY appears, silent. TOM looks uneasily about. He speaks in a whisper.

TOM: Quiet, the Men are listening…

SURGEON: I have known them go down well, and in the Morning be brought up Dead. I have sat by the Gratings and felt the Burst of Heat and Suffocation from their Rooms, as if I sat by a Fire in the Torrid Zone. It is the most horrid Sight I have ever seen. It is the Deformation of Flesh, a Vat of Blood and Mucus. It is the Boiling Coast…

TOM: (*To the CAPTAIN*) It's the knock on the Head.

BOSUN: This is Disobedience.

SURGEON: This is Hell!

The CAPTAIN hesitates, a moment of indecision. They watch him. He pushes aside the SURGEON and turns to the BOSUN.

CAPTAIN: Unlock the Armoury, Bosun. Give every Man his Gun. I'll wait no more on the Factories. A Bounty of One Guinea for every Negro captured, to be shared among the Crew. We sail tonight on the Land-wind.

TOM: This Action is illegal!

CAPTAIN: I am the Law here! Beyond my Word's the Coast — where there is no Law, only Banished Men. (*To the CREW*) Take Action to defend the Ship! We can Save ourselves and be out at Sea by Morning! One Guinea!

The CAPTAIN looks at the SLAVE slumped on the deck.

Clear that off the Deck. Make ready!

The ship's bell rings for action. The CAPTAIN goes. The CABIN-BOY gives his shoulder to the SURGEON and leads him away. The BOSUN takes hold of the chain and drags the SLAVE past TOM.

BOSUN: Look to me as we go. There's no one looking over our Shoulder when we set Foot there. No Classes of Men at all. Only those who don't know what Hell is, or don't believe in it. Or don't believe they're in it.

The BOSUN drags away the SLAVE.

TOM: We Steal, by Force.

He goes, the bell ringing.

The Raj Re-creation Big Tent

Rishi Dastidar

Imagine an elephant wearing a top hat, except you don't
    have to imagine it
as that is exactly what is happening in the Raj Re-creation
    Big Tent, arriving
on a blasted village heath near you quite soon, in a secure,
    socially-distanced
manner of course. I mean, who does not want to see an
    isosceles triangle that
thinks it's a continent but can't even manage to keep
    a dragon jaded instead
become all super-streamlined at warp speed into a future
    in which it incarnates
itself as progress maximised, and then wraps it all in
    licences and tops it with a

taxing bow? Meanwhile the audience in ones and ones
    chunters and guffaws under
Union Jack facemasks, pausing only to wonder how a bloke
    wearing a cloth of salt
had enough give to gab up the place, before stuffing some
    more coronation chicken
into their India Pale Ale and then wahey! What's a black hole,
    a famine or two, a
cricket test between friends? Odd how each of those started
    with the policy diktat:
what happens when they're not quite right for us? This is the
    thing about making the
world pink: you leave everything tender, scarred and flaking.
    Still, what a show eh?!

i am no less

Michelle Cahill

i am no acronym nor a hyphen, but Indian in blood,
colour, English in taste, tongue, Portuguese in spirit,
my Christianity disinherited, freed by dharma
unequal citizen, my skin measured by white space

i am not a subject to be read, bewildering, ironic
as the double tropes of conversion, patronised
no longer, my mind captive to identity, to borders,
dreaming this contrapuntal life, revived in words

more a pantomime girl standing with the damp pigeons
by the ashen river blowing incandescent bubbles
through metal loops of varied shapes and size
as the crowd veers past her, trying to hold just one

small things aggrieve if one is stateless, or weaponised
by the State that cares only if we are alive or dead
first memories are cherished. i remember the pavilion,
the merry-go-round, daffodils blooming, everything fizzing…

i would rather parachute from the skies, speak
a green rustle in dappled light, flare like autumn leaves,
be a child running circles around a fountain, as laughter
echoes in a square canopied by elders, giant trees

but a white boy teased me, someone else spat, so
that right here in this juvenile courtroom forever locked,
my colonial subject was stamped, doubly betrayed,
another lie leaking from the torn hymen of history —

because who on Earth is brave enough to admit
being half-caste is being someone else's armour?
they will mock and beam in approval, over and over,
so the true occasion for sanctuary is never born

we are not that different despite skin colour
or rank; who can take from us what we cherish most —
unmistakable as the dark ragged ink of the clouds,
or the scent of fresh air after rain? years melt,
the words vanishing in smog like Waterloo's taxis

i cannot say precisely why it feels quite so.
maybe the certainty of this diasporic un(making)
knowing the voice I have cherished belongs.
the city slinks, snow is mute, numb as my teeth
snow is the dirty white music of suffering

only to linger, to watch the muddy swans shuffle
from a polluted lake, joggers running, while lovers neck
and dogs defecate. to watch a row of brick houses
with twin chimneys reflect in the lake at twilight

there is a rickshaw parked outside Birkbeck, a bicycle
chained to the paling. the Tube is billowing with an ache
as commuters return to the brown-coloured suburbs,
as a woman in a sari ambles along the sinking jetty

trust me

Impulse

Aminatta Forna

At the top of the wall was a hole where a small vent had once been. And in the vent appeared a head, followed by the body of a bird. The bird pulled itself free and was joined by another and another, until a small flock of birds flew around Bimi's bedroom, and then into the hall and up the short flight of stairs to the sitting room of the apartment. There the birds settled on the backs of chairs and upon the curtain rail; one of the birds perched on top of the painting of a boy holding a giant sunflower. Bimi watched the birds with wonder, following them through the house. When she saw they meant no harm, she brewed a pot of coffee and turned on the radio. The birds were still, apart from the occasional rearrangement of a wing or alignment of a flight feather. Bimi opened a window in case the birds had somewhere else to be, and went to work, but when she returned they were all still there. So she drew a bath, and when the birds heard the sound of running water they appeared in the bathroom and sat on the toilet seat, the light fitting and the shower rail. One bird alighted on the towel rail but, finding it hot, hopped off and onto the side of the sink, which gave Bimi an idea. She filled the basin with cold water, and the birds took turns to bathe while Bimi lay in the bath and hummed, foam tickling the underside of her chin.

In the evening, before she settled down to watch television, she found a bag of sunflower seeds in the cupboard and put these out for the birds. There were carrots in the fridge, and she cut them up and added them to the tray, along with some pieces of apple. The birds formed a perfect circle around the food, dipping and rising like clockwork toys. At the sound of rain several birds lifted their heads to listen; only after a long time did they lower them again.

At work the day before, Bimi had looked out of the window to see a bird sitting on the sill next to her desk. It had a pleasant greyish-mauve colour, with black tail feathers, black eyes and a black spot on either side of its neck. The mourning dove – for that is what it was – looked up at Bimi and cocked its head, then turned and spent the rest of the morning regarding the view, like a bather standing at the edge of the sea.

At midday, Bimi was called into a meeting. She slipped on her shoes, smoothed her skirt. In the meeting, she watched a presentation by the Chief Data Officer. On a large screen, charts flowed into one another and merged with images that rolled into films. Afterwards there was a discussion. Bimi raised a hand, but when nobody called on her, she spoke suddenly and very loudly. A man, who was Bimi's boss and the boss of everyone in the room, turned to look at her. The Chief Data Officer shrugged and said, 'But the numbers.' The man who was Bimi's boss sighed loudly: 'I think we're done here.' When the meeting broke up, Bimi slid a stapler from his desk into her jacket pocket.

Later, the stapler sitting on a low coffee table in front of her, Bimi stretched out her legs. The stapler looked like a gleaming green crocodile. 'Well, Bimi?' said her therapist. They had been together in the room for an hour. But Bimi did not answer. She picked up the crocodile and placed it in her handbag.

At home she found a cat waiting outside her door, a cat she thought she recognised as belonging to someone in the apartment block. When she opened the door the cat paced inside, its head low, settled with its back to a radiator and extended a leg like a hirsute, shrunken yoga instructor. Bimi put down a saucer of milk and went to see if the birds were still in the bathroom, which they were, including the mourning dove. She was rapidly becoming familiar with the flock, for the reason that the flock – of precisely eleven birds – was composed of different species. She put out a hand and the dove flew and alighted there; another bird settled on her shoulder and, followed by the remainder of the flock, she led them to the front room to meet the cat.

Late that night came the sound of her doorbell. Bimi, who expected nobody, looked out into the street, but the street was empty, puddles of rainwater collecting at the entrance to the building. When she turned around, the birds and the cat were looking at her. 'Okay, okay,' said Bimi. She took the stairs and opened the front door. There sat a trio of dogs, soaking. Bimi picked up the smallest of the dogs and the others followed. After she had towelled the dogs with a dishcloth, she put down some water. She searched the fridge for something suitable — but, alas, the fridge was bare, so she telephoned for a pizza.

'Your dog's waiting to get in,' said the delivery man. The dog was small with dainty black paws, a pointed face with orange eyes and a thick coat the same colour as its eyes. Bimi held out her hand for the pizza. 'Thanks,' she said. She took the lift back upstairs. At the last moment, a young man carrying a silver scooter entered just as the door was closing. The young man lowered his hood, pushed a hand through his damp hair and, looking down at the dog, said, 'Rad!'

Inside the apartment Bimi fetched nuts and fruit for the birds, and shared out the pizza. The animals ate and watched the rain as it beat against the window. Drops somersaulted from the sky, Bimi saw them, in her mind's eye, catch in the gutters and hurtle onwards until they joined many millions more drops, waters now, that lay with deceptive calm as they rose and rose.

Lunchtime the next day, and people hurried out into the rain for sandwiches, sushi and paper cups of burning soup. Bimi watched the man who was her boss from the other side of the glass. He was moving random papers on his desk and opening and closing drawers. She watched him step out of his office, a sheaf of papers in his hand; finally, he alighted upon a stapler on a desk, applied it to the papers in his hand and returned with both papers and stapler to his office. Bimi rose and knocked on his door. He was sitting at his desk with three piles of paper in front of him; he waved Bimi in as he picked up one of the piles and threw it in the bin.

'What are those?' asked Bimi.

'Applications for the new position,' said the man who was her boss. He removed his reading glasses, laid them at the edge of his desk and extended a hand.

Bimi wondered whose applications he had thrown away. She handed him a report. Bimi didn't agree with some of the things that were written in the report, though she had done as she'd been asked and dutifully corrected the grammar and punctuation. She didn't think everybody in the world wanted a banana slicer or kneepads for their baby, an indoor mushroom farm, an electric egg cooker capable of boiling twelve eggs, outerwear for dogs or even a robot vacuum cleaner — though Bimi herself would not mind owning one of those. She said none of this. Instead she palmed her boss's reading glasses from his desk.

'It is a question of impulse control,' said Bimi's therapist. 'There are some medications we could try.' Bimi was wearing the glasses, through which the form of her therapist was blurry and her movements vague. Bimi looked at her own hand, moving it forward and back from her nose.

'Would you stop that, please?'

Bimi put her hand on her lap, where it lay curled like a sleeping creature.

'Have you been trying the exercises I gave you to help with self-control?'

Bimi looked at her therapist from over the top of the glasses.

Bimi didn't take things from shops or from the houses of friends or from libraries. Presently, in fact, she only removed items from the desk of the man who was her boss. Before that, she had taken items from her father: a cufflink, nail clippers, a business card belonging to somebody he had just met. Other times, she had merely moved his things around the house; his cigarette lighter she'd put in the fridge more than once. One day, Bimi's brother found her trove of items hidden at the back of a drawer. On the scale of crimes and misdemeanours, nobody had stopped to ask why he had been rifling through her belongings in the first place. Bimi's father paid for her therapist because, he said, he did not wish to see his daughter in handcuffs, and Bimi removed a single piece from a jigsaw puzzle of the solar system her brother had laid out on the dining room table.

The animals were waiting in a semi-circle around the door like a welcome committee when Bimi came home. She fashioned leads for the dogs from various belts. Once down in the street, the birds flew overhead and the cat brought up the rear. It had never stopped raining and the streets were darkening and quiet. A man dashed past holding a newspaper over his head. A child standing outside a shop holding a transparent umbrella turned her face towards Bimi, as if to the moon, following the arc of the birds that floated above and around Bimi's head and shoulders with an index finger. Bimi raised one finger at the child, gave a single unsmiling nod, as though exchanging a secret sign.

They made their way to the small park, a strip of grass alongside the railway embankment, upon which greasy paper bags and beer cans bloomed like filthy flowers. The dogs departed in different directions, noses to the ground, except for the one with the sharp face and black paws, which jumped, with unexpected agility, up on a wall and ran along the top before descending the other side. Bimi sat in the rain for fifteen minutes. She had come out without an umbrella or a coat; she still had on the dress she had worn to the office. Another time, she might have worried about what the water was doing to the fabric; instead she sat and waited for the animals to return, and when they did she rose and they all moved as one. On her way back, a man on a silver scooter floated by, stopped and skated back past her. 'Hold on there, *chica*,' he called. 'You're leaving a man on the battlefield.' And Bimi noticed, for the first time, a fat squirrel waddling behind her. The man, who Bimi now recognised as the young man from the lift the day before, picked up the squirrel, set it on the silver scooter and began to push it. He walked Bimi to her door and handed her the squirrel. 'Thank you,' said Bimi.

In the apartment, Bimi noticed that there were now two pointy-faced dogs. There was an air of expectancy about all the creatures as they watched her or watched the rain. Bimi turned on the television and immediately the room was filled with shouts. The sudden noise caught everyone's attention, even that of the mouse sitting on Bimi's foot thoughtfully chewing her shoelace. Water poured down the outside of the glass; it had even begun to pool on the inside sill and was running down the wall. When she turned back to the television there was the FTSE, a saw-toothed downward gash. Now Bimi understood.

Most days, on her way to the train station, Bimi walked past a place housed beneath the railway arches that hired out camper vans. The camper vans were older models, the original VWs, and were painted in gaudy colours and covered in art made to look like graffiti, or perhaps vice versa. A few were for sale. Bimi went over her calculations; she had lived simply for many years. She knocked on the door of the office, itself housed in a camper van standing on bricks. The door opened and a young man ducked his head out. It was the owner of the silver scooter. He grinned.

'Hi,' said Bimi, not smiling because she felt she didn't really know him that well. 'I need a camper van.'

'Sure thing, *chica*,' said the young man. 'They're pretty much all the same, whichever one you like the look of.'

'I want to buy one,' Bimi pointed at two that were for sale.

The young man tilted his head to one side and scratched his chin and put out his hand. 'I'm Alex.'

The purchase of the camper van meant Bimi was late for work. The lift at the office was out of order, so she had to take the stairs. She noticed the hall carpet was damp. Water was pouring in through several holes in the office ceiling. Her colleagues scurried to and fro, positioning metal bins, shaking drops from leaves of paper. Someone was drying contracts with a hair dryer. The man who was her boss looked at her and said: 'Fetch a mop or something, for God's sake!'

Bimi went out into the hall, walked past the cupboard where the janitor kept her supplies, down the stairs and through the front door. At home, the animals waited. Bimi began to load them into the camper van, starting with the dogs, the cat and the birds. She closed the door and turned to find the squirrel and the mouse riding the silver scooter, like the homecoming king and queen, pushed by Alex.

'Your door was open,' he said.

'Thank you,' said Bimi.

'Where are you headed?'

Bimi glanced at the sky, rain drops landing on her cheeks. 'North,' she said.

Bimi climbed into her camper van, turned the key and then the wheel, and pulled out. As she depressed the accelerator the van began to gather speed, and the dove, perched on the headrest of the passenger seat, flapped its wings vigorously. The cat shot backwards. A dog pushed its snout over her shoulder and its breath fogged the window. Bimi eased off the accelerator and lowered the window so the dog could stick its head out. In the mirror she saw Alex on his silver scooter, speeding after the van. She turned to the pointy-faced dog sitting on the passenger seat. It returned her gaze and then turned resolutely back to stare through the windscreen. The dog barked. Bimi put her foot down.

We Wait

Rafeef Ziadah

This mourning stretches into
a visa line across Damascus to Athens.
And the horizon still unforgiving.

We hold open passports and scars.
There are legal documents to trace our goodbyes.
There are suitcases stuffed with ash.

Across the gates they look beyond us.

The line wraps neatly around the corner,
as we wait and wait.

We're not quite right.
The smell of escape in our bones.
Our teeth not shiny enough.

This mourning continues to stretch
into visa lines unforgiving and absolute.
Head down in surrender.
No fig trees or hills to hold us.
We run from earth to water,
to silent skies.

But we're not quite right:
for the soldier who watches gates,
the official who inspects,
the welfare officer who checks
and double checks
how an extra loaf of bread
made its way to our table.

Across the gates they look beyond us.
And we wait and wait.

VI love

'She draws a fine line of blood about three centimetres long'

The Woman Who Bought a Cloak

Selina Tusitala Marsh

Cape Kidnappers sits on the east coast of the North Island of Aotearoa New Zealand. It is notoriously named after an incident that occurred in 1769, during Cook's first voyage. Taiata, the Tahitian servant of Tupia, Cook's navigator and interpreter, was seized by some Māori during a botched trading attempt. We don't know what went wrong, only that Taiata was taken as collateral. Cook's response was certainly the worst kidnapping retrieval plan ever: cannonball the *waka* and everyone in it, Taiata included — except he jumped *waka* and escaped.

Cape Kidnappers is also the site of one of the country's most renowned luxury lodges. I have been invited to speak to thirty Australians, wealthy lovers of literature, on a leg of their literary tour. I weighed up the invitation; it would cost me yet another weekend away from my family and from my own much-needed recuperative time. But the organisation pays generously, covering all expenses, including two nights at the lodge. A quick Google search made my decision. I would be paid to give myself a mini-retreat. I'd been trying to cultivate a habit of self-care during – not just after – work, because 'after' seldom happens. This gig would do nicely.

After gourmet mussel fritters, soft venison with roast beetroot and feta salad and tempura vegetables on the side, my talk and performance go down as smoothly as the Cloudy Bay bubbles. I stand against a dramatic panoramic view of Te Mata Peak and the slow wending Tukituki river. They laugh, some cry, there is a flurry of questions. My message – to tell your tale or someone else will … or won't – the perfect balance of sweet and tart to finish off the meal.

When I board the coach back to the lodge, I find myself in the midst of a seat-bidding frenzy.

'Sit with me!'

'There's room here!'

Some members of this book group have made this annual excursion together for years. Every year another beautiful destination is selected, tickets and tours paid for, writers booked and a week-long retreat in Ubud or Milan planned.

There's a tug on my arm. I recognise the woman who had shouted at me the day before. Wanting to make the most of the last few hours of daylight, I'd dumped my bags in the room, changed into my running gear and set out on a complimentary mountain bike. I was in search of Te Kauwae-a-Māui, 'the fishhook of Māui', which he used to fish up the North Island — otherwise known as Te Ika-a-Māui, 'the fish of Māui'. Gotta love that demi-god's chutzpah!

Making it to the most south-eastern point of the peninsula is thrilling. The terrain is vertical in some places. The intermittent baaahs from sheep dotting the hills is the only other sound apart from my tyres scrunching on the gravel road and the squeal of brakes echoing through the carved-out valley walls. When I reach the headland, I glimpse the sharp tip of the ancient fishhook rising from the seas. Caught. I swivel around to race against the dark. I refuse to push the lodge GPS button that would summon a cushy white golf cart to retrieve me.

By the time I reach the steep, looping driveway to the lodge, I'm standing and pedalling in slow motion, sweating in my merino.

'Just push the button, dear!' A woman shouts behind me.

I turn around.

'Thanks, but I'm already here!' I come to a sticky, huffing stop. The woman breezes up alongside me. She removes her helmet.

'Oh, you've got a real bike! Sorry, thought you had an e-bike, same as ours!' She clasps my arm, laughing. I smile back.

'I earned those hills.'

'Indeed, you did — fabulous. See you around!'

Rich people. They're not so bad.

Back on the coach, the same woman clasps my arm.

'Sit next to me, my dear, I need your advice!'

Another woman across the aisle frowns at this blatant physical redirection.

The woman pats my arm.

'Now, you're the expert and I need your advice. You said, "Tell your tale or someone else will … or won't." Well, I have a tale, but I don't know if I should tell it.'

The woman tells me about her visit to the Serengeti five years earlier. She and her husband are seasoned travellers, preferring tailor-made, personalised tours to experience the real life of a place. They want to experience this beautiful and culturally rich world in a genuine way. Their guide took them to a Maasai village. She leans into me, gripping my arm like an old girlfriend.

'I was walking through their camp and then I see her from behind. The most beautiful, statuesque woman in front of me wearing the most wondrous cloak. Its beads were swaying with the regal to-ing and fro-ing of her body. The colours, the textures against her shining black skin were mesmerising. I still see it now so vividly – the colours, the rhythm – hypnotic.'

The woman now has both hands swaying in front of her, mimicking the slow sashay of this cloak, her eyes round with worship.

'I wanted to reach out and touch it, to touch her. Instead, I found myself putting my hand on her shoulder. The woman spins around, bringing her brood to a halt. Her four small sons look up at me. Oh, she was just so beautiful!'

I bite down on my lip.

'Before I know it, I'm saying, "Can I buy your cloak?"'

I bite down harder.

'Of course, our guide had to interpret. I've never offered to buy things off people's backs. But this cloak, it was magical. I had no choice!'

The Maasai woman did, though.

'"Not for sale," she replies through the interpreter.' The woman leans into me, her hand vice-gripping my knee. 'I say, through the interpreter, of course, "There's no pressure!

I didn't mean to offend. It's just that your cloak is the most beautiful thing I've ever seen. I just had this immediate physical response to it."'

It turned out the intricately beaded animal skin was a wedding cloak, and very old. Each bead symbolised a tribal marriage, and is handsewn into the skin. Older glass, stone or shell beads began high up on the cloak. More recent weddings were marked with shiny plastic beads lower down the back.

The woman was permitted to take photos, though. Of the Maasai woman. Of her cloak. Of the beads shimmering on her back as she walked away. Of her sons trailing behind her.

'Then I forgot completely about it … until the next day.'

The woman and her husband had just finished breakfast and were heading towards the tour car when she saw a tall, slim boy standing outside their hotel. She recognised him from the day before.

'She will sell,' he says to the interpreter.

'Well, I didn't know what to say. I'd quite put it out of my mind. I wasn't too sure I wanted it now, it was a kind of spur-of-the-moment thing. I'd been so captivated by the colours, the movement, the woman herself. But now here was one of her sons, waiting to take us.'

They drove back to the Maasai camp. The woman bought the cloak.

'What made her change her mind?' I ask.

'The interpreter told me that the money would pay the school fees for her children for two years. "Well," I thought, "anything to help." I've sent them care packages over the years.'

The woman shipped the cloak back to Sydney and placed it on a mannequin displayed in the drawing room. Behind it she erected a framed photo of the Maasai woman wearing it. She wore it twice herself. For five years, she felt the joy of it every time she passed through the drawing room.

Until the mould appeared.

The Canberra restorer specialising in African artefacts couldn't believe what she had in front of her.

'The specialist – she knows her stuff, believe you me – told me how rare Maasai wedding cloaks are, especially one as pristine as this. She's never seen one as intricate, as old as this one, not even in museums! Frankly, she was shocked at how casually I'd shipped it across the country.'

The skin was drying out. It was no longer being worn daily, no longer absorbing the natural oils of human skin. Out of its natural environment, it began dying.

'I asked the restorer if I should return it to Africa.'

'God, no!' The restorer replied. 'There are only a handful of these in existence. We would lose it! Who would keep it for generations to come?'

The woman had bought the cloak for US $200. She paid AUS $2,000 to have the mould removed. She received strict instructions on its care: it must not be displayed in the open air, nor in unfiltered sunlight. It must be kept on a special temperature-controlled, light-modified display table. Until the table was ready, it would need to be stored in a custom-made 1.5 metre x 1 metre box, draped over a specially made bodice.

'But where to put it, Sel? The box is awkwardly big. At the moment it's under the bed in one of the guest rooms.'

I look at the woman and exhale.

'You see my dilemma. Do I tell its tale? If I return it, who will ever hear it? Maybe it wants to go back to its owner. But how will I ever find her? It's my responsibility now. Well? What do you think?'

I inhale and tell her this story:

The Women Who Bought a Cloak

We call ourselves 'the Aunties'. We are Dames and Officers of the New Zealand Order of Merit. We are mothers and sisters. We are doctors and artists, researchers and activists. We are students and corporate executives. We are leaders and supporters; we are old, we are young. We are 165 New Zealand women and we are buying a cloak to place around the shoulders of our prime minister, Jacinda Ardern. We want her to know that we are her tribe. That we've got her back. That's what aunties do. No special occasion. No event to be marked and strictly no press. Just arms around an extraordinary woman, leading at an extraordinary time. Someone who embodies the zeitgeist of our nation: a country that prides itself on what its 'can do-will do' farming kiwi culture calls a No. 8 wire mentality, where a piece of wire can be bent to fix anything from a broken fence to a malfunctioning engine. A nation that does things differently. Post-Christchurch massacre and pre-COVID.

The Aunties recognise the deep strength, tenacity and high level of task-switching required to lead this nation. Prime Minister Ardern is the thirty-nine-year-old mother of our nation and of a two-year-old daughter; she is only the second world leader to have given birth while in office. She is the first non-Muslim woman leader to wear a hijab and have her image projected on the tallest building in the world, the Burj Khalifa. She is the first New Zealand prime minister to use words such as 'kindness' and 'care' in public and to *mean* it, infusing these words into policy. As mothers, sisters, daughters, grandmothers and granddaughters, we imagine the cost.

We each put NZD \$150 in the kitty to make Jacinda her own *korowai*, her own feathered Māori cloak. She wore a borrowed one for her visit to the Queen. This *korowai* will be woven for her by the master weavers Matekino Lawless and her daughter, Christina Wirihana. They are weaving with the rarest of feathers — kiwi. All of us are present in spirit, as each feather is stitched in.

I suggest to Jo, Chief Aunty, that our literal cloaking of our prime minister extends to our metaphorical cloaking of her: 'Let's weave our words into the lining of the *korowai*.'

I ask each woman to complete the line *I cloak you in …* Jacinda can wear the *korowai* out in public. Then, perhaps, when no one is looking, perhaps during times when strength, courage and love are most needed, perhaps when she feels alone or broken or disillusioned, she will turn her cloak inside out and place our lines of womanist love, strength and lineage around her shoulders.

I weave the words of 165 women together to create a *korowai* poem. Sewing it into the lining of the delicate garment proves too difficult, so on 6 December 2019, in Ōrākei Marae, outside Auckland, in front of 165 women, Jacinda is presented with her *korowai* along with a full-size framed print of the poem. Standing between Jacinda on the *paepae* (forecourt) of the *marae* – the sacred communal space – and the women gathered on the lawn, I perform the poem on their behalf. I turn it into an interactive performance, with the women repeating the first part of each line at my signal. One hundred and sixty-five voices rise in unison and say: 'I cloak you in …' after which I complete the line. An excerpt follows:

I cloak you in tradition, each strand tells a story
I cloak you in resilience, a beauteous *pōhutukawa*
I cloak you in iron sand, salt spray and *toetoe*
We cloak you in support, a women-woven web

I cloak you in birdsong, when the day is long, difficult
I cloak you in courage, to steer our *waka* by the stars
I cloak you in *aroha*, woven with *manaakitanga, tikanga* and
      wairua
We cloak you in *ngākau pono*, loyalty, of grace known

I cloak you in *aroha, awhi* and gratitude
I cloak you in your imperfections; let them shine for all to
      see
I cloak you in *mana moana*, to connect you to the vitality and
      power of Oceania
We cloak you in poetry, the flame-red hibiscus behind your
      ear.

The mesmerising power of the rhythmic chant sweeps over us, moving us in currents of emotion. Tears roll down Jacinda's cheeks. Tears roll down ours. In this moment, we are a tribe. We are making history. Holding this history. Each feather sewn, each *muka* pattern woven, holds a story of our interwovenness, our connection. Each line of poetry, a bead of belonging.

*

'So, should I frame it, then?' asks the woman.
    'Not quite,' I reply and, like Taiata, jump *waka*.

Notes & Glossary

Deep appreciation to Founding Aunties Jo Brosnahan and Anne Salmond; and to Eddy Royal, Jacinda's bestie.

Culturally contextualised understandings of words can be found at: https://maoridictionary.co.nz/

Aroha: love
Awhi: embrace
Korowai: cloak
Manaakitanga: hospitality
Ngākau pono: loyalty
Mana moana: authority over the sea and lakes
Muka: prepared flax fibre
Ōrākei Marae: tribal meeting ground for the iwi of Ngāti Whātua
    o Ōrākei
Pōhutukawa: New Zealand Christmas tree
Tikanga: correct procedure
Toetoe: thatch of rushes
Waka: canoe
Wairua: spirit

The Pilgrimage

Amina Atiq

We kissed at the border
but you stole my heart, offering it to Najran –

but I was too young
to understand this warfare-
love story when my tongue
is tied to this English home;
but we lose ourselves
in our peculiar summer pilgrimages
to a place elsewhere.

Only the diaspora crossed-legged
children understand, slurring
basic Arabic letters across the
cabinet classroom –
your teacher tall as you,
pointing her nose upwards:

*'Never lose yourself in this place
even if you lose yourself.'*

These children daydream
abstract checkpoints of stick men
in uniform, confessing
to the moon with their flags
stuck upright, we search
for home in our radical love letters
across the 'English' Channel pushing
the French waters,
when the lifeguard sleeps

we recreate the kiss at the border
rotted in abandonment,
stuttering its national anthem
it turns in its grave
and the invaders prowling
in our summer journeys
is a love story missing –

the school bell rings,
the children unpack
their tuna butties
and SMART PRICE orange juice,
speaking over each other
in their second language
with their mouths full,
they suck the life out of them
straws, turning sideways.

Knot

Leone Ross

Diana hadn't intended to steal the knot out of the young woman's belly. She took the knot on a whim; up early, tiptoeing past her son Gabriel's bedroom, trying not to creak – her hips or the floorboards – pulling on thick socks and bright blue wellies, smoothing her hair into a bun and stuffing it under one of Jonathan's snug olive-green caps. It was Gabe's first time home from university and the first young woman he'd ever had to stay.

There were so many things *wrong* with the thieving moment. Gabe's barely-open bedroom door, Diana's inability to resist looking in at the sleeping couple, the stab she'd been feeling since yesterday afternoon, *stab-stab-stab* since they'd arrived. She hadn't wanted to endure the sight of her son, lying on his side, his shoulder bare in lemonade light, the rest of him mercifully tucked under the duvet, cupping a woman to his body, but she couldn't help staring, regardless.

The girl's head rested on Gabriel's bicep. Her arms were crossed, like embracing herself, and they were holding hands. Susan, that was her name. She'd kicked off the duvet and so she lay naked, slumbering untroubled, as if Gabriel alone made the house and the world warm enough. Diana thought how unfamiliar this body was: nipples so far apart, one dangling towards her navel, everything terribly pendulous. Diana had always been small-breasted, even during pregnancy. The girl's belly was big enough to cover her pudenda, sparing the ultimate embarrassment but, as Diana looked closer, she'd realised there was a knot right there. She could see it through the stomach's stretched and transparent skin. The quivering knot reminded her of thickly-woven grey and white wool, turned in on itself, wrapped over and over, until the whole was the size of a small but formidable puppy.

Diana knew dogs; she'd had so many. It was one of the reasons she'd gotten up for a morning walk for years. But their last dog, an old, soft Bichon Frisé called Mister Walcott, had died last summer. They were certain to get another one, but Jonathan had been travelling and Gabe had to be packed off to university, and a new puppy was a mammoth undertaking; even a shelter mid-life doggy would need such attention.

Before she quite knew what she was doing, Diana clicked her right fingers and whistled low under her breath.

'Hey boy … hey boy.'

The knot wriggled delightedly. Diana scowled. Perfectly ordinary Susan, who had arrived at her house last night and lit a bomb under her entire existence. Diana saw that she'd carefully stored her engagement ring on the bedside table, close, so that she could seize it when she woke, jam it on her finger again, jam it into Diana's eye, both eyes, like a hot needle.

The knot whined.

'Come on, boy,' softly patting her hip.

The knot pulled itself free from Susan's abdomen, like sticking plaster. Diana didn't stop to worry whether the young woman's internal organs were exposed to the cold air or bleeding. It would serve her right.

They left the house together, knot slipping joyfully down the rainy front steps, raindrops gathering on Diana's bifocals like tears. She pulled her coat tighter, the gold and green tattoo on her left shoulder glimmering under the porch light.

*

She'd expected to be happy and welcoming the first time Gabe brought a girlfriend home; she wasn't a young mother, but she could be of help to a girl, she thought. Nurturing, or wise. She might provide some kind of context, be helpful. Introduce her around a bit, lunch or shopping, of course, and something more robust if Gabe married one day. As a family, they did a lot of philanthropic work, locally and abroad. She made the occasional speech. Recently she'd done a debate for charity, arguing why it was unhelpful to talk about 'Africa' when you were trying to help the particularity of Nigeria or Ghana.

Diana had asked the cleaner to prepare the third bedroom for Gabe's arrival, the double ensuite. Not the room with two single beds — something a diplomatic friend had suggested. She was determined to respect the couple's adulthood. But when she heard the crunching sound of her husband's car back from the train station, pulling into the gravel drive and settling in the garage, and the sound of talking and laughing, she felt unexpectedly weary, and leaned her forehead against the cool, stippled kitchen wall before going out into the hall.

She knew before she met the girl; she knew in her heart what was coming. She wished for the honest bounce of a dog around her ankles, so she and the stranger walking towards her could become entangled in the canine glee, in that way of dog lovers — *ah, he's a lovely one, what's his name? Breed? Come here, lovely. How long have you had him? Looks to be … three or so?*

She had no idea whether or not Susan liked dogs. Susan had several tattoos and a silver nose ring, but they'd had the good sense to arrive without her engagement ring on show. Thinking back, Diana was pretty sure that she was the only one who didn't know, on that cold, dog-less doorstep, her husband seeking her eyes and smiling far too wide. *Can Pa pick us up at the station?* Gabriel had asked. Of course he wanted his father. To talk about how to handle his mother.

Mamma won't like it.

She'll be fine, Gabriel.

'Welcome,' she said, 'welcome, ah.' Reached out to hug her tall, good looking, creamy boy to her body, Gabriel with his always-glittering black eyes; and then this Susan, her eyes glittering too, head up, back straight, smiling.

The girl was not anxious at all. She reached out to clasp Diana's hands, with her fat black self, and she was just as calm as the lake down by the Peter Hunt Row, and near as tall as her son.

Diana nearly drew back.

The confident young woman's jeans were far too tight for this occasion and she had clipped and sensible nails, and she was squeezing Diana's palms almost as if *she* was welcoming *her*.

Enter the first *stab-stab* of fury.

*

Dinner was agreeable. She'd hired a local chef. A starter of sea bass and assorted bright greens, a white bean cassoulet with clams and braised pig trotter. Susan stared at the plump, open clams on her plate, brow knit. Should she gesture her towards the fish cutlery? Indicate the shells weren't edible? Surely not.

Susan glanced up. Diana delicately placed a clam in her mouth, so the girl could follow suit. Susan winked and mimicked her. They chewed together. Diana felt her tongue, heavy in her mouth. Rudderless.

'Mamma,' Gabriel said. He reached out for Susan's hand and squeezed it. When he was a little boy he'd instinctively guard the shyest child. Diana stole a glance at Jonathan, who was watching his son carefully.

'Mamma,' said Gabe. 'We.'

We. Oh, it was *we*, was it?

We.

Susan beamed: an oily, happy mass of tight clothes at her table.

*

Later, making ready for bed, her husband could not stop smiling, a jack-in-the-box. She stood by the nightstand, one hand on her hip, left foot tapping. Jonathan drew her into the thick duvet, soothing and stroking.

'She's good, Oluyemi. Can you not see she's a good girl?'

She bit her lip not to cry.

'Of all evenings, *now* you choose to call me that?'

He stroked her face, the shoulder tattoo, fingers trailing. 'Sometimes I like to call you by the name your mother gave you, Di.'

She grunted. He was such an agreeable companion. Of her excellent taste in him she was sure, if nothing else in this world. Even when other things were sinking, spraying, cracking, drowning, when she was fattened with tears. But he was wrong about this girl. This Susan who looked her in the face, like she didn't know the pull of oceans.

*

The knot that lived in Susan's stomach whickered along beside her, trailing through puddles, practically wagging.

'Morning, Diana!' One of her young, fashionable neighbours whizzing past, out for a jog, turning back, waving enthusiastically. 'Lovely new pup. Old English Sheepie! I thought you might choose something more exotic than that!'

People were fools the minute you let them be fools.

The knot rolled on, like a fluffy tumbleweed, keeping to her heel as she walked briskly towards the river path. Once they reached the water, the knot chased up and down the bank, writhing joyfully at the ducks and geese. It was entirely silent, but she could imagine it barking; the ducks fled, quacking, outraged. The knot looked ready to follow on, so Diana picked it up to prevent watery calamity.

Up close and in good light, the knot was beautiful: it was dangled with gold beads, ruby beads, tiger amber beads, heavy and opulent things, as if scattered with brightly coloured eyeballs. For all its bounce, it was an old knot. There was something about its heft and steady breathing that suggested decades. No, no, centuries. Perhaps it had been a gift to the girl. A family heirloom from ancestors.

She walked on, cradling the belly-knot against her shoulder. It was hot and bristly. Did it get thirsty? Did you feed a knot? Did it need care and attention? It seemed healthy. Despite all evidence to the contrary, its presence must mean that Susan was afraid. Why else might a person carry a knot in their belly? She was surprised at her own relief; yes, let the girl be terrified. It was *appropriate*. She recalled her own mother-in-law, Shelagh, decades ago, her well-preserved face pulled in half when Jonathan announced their engagement, two years into medical school. Shelagh's brittle alarm, even though they had done everything just right: a long courting period, her nursing degree abandoned, her own impeccable manners, her hair ironed straight — the tattoo, her one blushing indiscretion, carefully hidden. There were long arguments into the night amongst the adults about their future. Jonathan, her dear heart, could not be moved in his resolve and, in her quiet way, neither could she.

But she had been terrified.

The knot rolled up a tree, spraying buttery leaves and scarlet berries; before she could remonstrate, it rolled down again, *skip-hop-bump*. Was it shrinking?

She remembered her first Sunday in church with her mother-in-law; Shelagh's unashamed prayer that her grandchildren wouldn't be dark-skinned.

Diana made kissing noises to pull the knot back towards her and they carried along down the river bank.

*

She and Susan prepared a pot of tea together as the evening darkened; Jonathan liked a biscuit and cheese at 7.30. She'd sent the waiting staff home deliberately, but even as Susan filled the kettle and she searched for crockery, she regretted this small decision, discomfited by the sheer expanse of the flesh before her. Susan had changed into a thin, bright orange wraparound dress and open-toed sandals, exposing cleavage and matching silvery fingers and toes. Three piercings in one ear, seven in the other; the nose, the nose.

'There's another piercing down below,' said Susan, following her eyes, twitching her hips and laughing, then flapping her hands. 'No, I'm *joking*, man! Gabe, I freaked your mum out!'

The knot bounced into a puddle, rolled out again and shook itself. The river water rustled past, clearer than she remembered it ever being. She could see the river stones in great detail, a small blue shoe left back by some strange and careless child, fish blooping by, two cormorants stalking through.

The knot wound around her legs, snuffling.

The task was to make it bigger, decided Diana. Yes, she could find a way to do that. Perhaps if the knot in Susan's stomach got bigger, she would go away.

*

The second morning she was up even earlier than usual. Jonathan woke with her and wanted to make love, but she said she wasn't in the mood, so he pleased himself by stroking long fingers down her hip and masturbating idly. Soon he fell asleep again, curled exaggeratedly on his side of the bed, as if she smelled, or he was suddenly afraid. She nudged a pillow under his skull and slipped out.

This time the knot wrenched itself free from Susan's sleeping belly and rolled towards her, whimpering. Diana was touched despite herself, watching the knot head out into the dawn and towards the river.

Down on the wet soil she crouched, like old women did in older and wiser places, and fed the knot from her backpack. The knot glistened and pulsated and chomped. She fed it fennel and dark chocolate florentines, tangerines, a bowl of oysters, a head of fresh dew-drunk lettuce from her own garden, a whole bottle of Veuve Clicquot, complete with flutes. She fed it pieces of her old school reports, Jonathan's accounts from last year and a bar of purple lavender soap. She fed it the other pillow from her bed and a book about mermaids that her three-year-old niece had left in the conservatory, and three pairs of earrings she hadn't worn for more than a year, and then the insurance papers for the same earrings.

The knot ate rapidly, its furry grey and white sides heaving. It seemed happy, its appetite prodigious, but it didn't seem to be expanding, so she fed it nine water balloons; she had intended ten, but one burst with too much river water.

*

The family went for a long walk that afternoon, driving first then parking and trailing into the dappled summer woods. Diana watched Susan chattering with the men and striding through ferns and vines on the path, laughing at a surprised fox, a surprised moorhen, a surprised squirrel. They played a memory game of lists that became too complicated as the sun blazed down on the still-damp trees. The young woman stopped on the path more frequently as time passed, grimacing and rubbing her lower stomach. She noticed Diana watching her.

'Knickers too tight,' she joked. Gabriel burst into laughter and reached out to gently rub the offending belly. Diana smiled tightly and walked on ahead. She put her fingers in her ears to block out the tinkle of their laughter. Gabriel promised if the pain got worse, he'd carry her home.

'You'd put your back out,' Diana muttered under her breath.

Jonathan glared. 'Shh, they'll hear you.'

'Mm.'

'Now why would you say such a thing?'

They found the brink of a wide lake, spread two large purple blankets and unpacked a picnic. Diana had ordered from the best local service: homemade onion and balsamic sourdough bread with churned butter, smoked ham hock, yellow split pea purée with slow-roasted tomatoes and caramelised onions, yellow potatoes tossed in pesto, Cornish crab stuffed into bright blue crab shells, mozzarella chunks, pork and stilton pie with pickled onion slices, caramel popcorn, chocolate fondants that bled unexpectedly tart strawberry gooiness.

Gabriel poured Susan a glass of prosecco and orange juice.

'Maybe not right now,' said Susan. 'I must have eaten something bad last night.' Diana rolled her eyes. She'd been hosted for two days; so rude to suggest anything *she'd* served had made her ill.

'Mum, has this got onions in it?' said Gabriel. 'I did tell you Suse was allergic. And she doesn't really eat pork.'

'Gabe, it doesn't matter,' said Susan. Her top lip sweated. She lay back on Gabriel's chest, taking up most of one of the blankets. Jonathan put his hand on her forehead. Diana could see the edges of the knot pulsating gently through her belly-skin; it was swelling. She hid a smile.

'We can stay here for a while, see if you feel better,' said Jonathan. He poured a cup of peppermint tea to settle her nausea. Susan said he was very kind.

Diana glared at the fussing men. The sun poured down from a cloudless, brilliant sky. She imagined the heat making the girl stink. She imagined her born in a poor place — a tenement yard, a slum, a jungle. A feral thing.

Gabriel fanned Susan slowly.

'I love summer,' said Susan. She belched. 'I'm going to be *so* black when I get back.'

Jonathan handed Diana a glass of prosecco. She drank furiously, her head damp and sore.

*

The afternoon beat on: the rest of them ate the very good food; Susan seemed to improve. There was no hurry. The men calmed. They played Scrabble. Gabriel won with *quetzals*, placing all seven letters on his rack, with the 'q' and the 's' on triple word score squares and the 'z' on a double letter score.

'Three hundred annnnnd seventy-four!' yelped Susan. 'You bastard. I was going to play eight, Gabe. Eight. *Ouch.*' She hiccupped.

'*Quetzal*, the national bird of Guatemala,' said Jonathan. 'I seem to recall you playing that before. You were about eleven.'

After the Scrabble game, the couple wandered off around the edge of the lake and were gone for a while. Diana pretended to doze in the heat, ignoring Jonathan's attempts at conversation.

'Is there something you see or know that I don't?' asked Jonathan. 'You seem so displeased.'

She sat up. 'He's *marrying*, Jonathan. He. Is. Nineteen.'

'You were nineteen.'

'That's different.'

'How so? Do you think she's pregnant?'

'Not *yet*. Her kind.'

'I'll have a word with Gabriel, make sure he's taking care.' Her husband paused. '"Her *kind*", Diana. You…'

'What about me?'

'Come, now, Di. *My* mother, all pale and wan. Drooping like a weeping willow.'

She rolled over, sat up and, shielding her eyes, began to pack the picnic basket.

Susan returned, rubbing and rubbing her mouth. The knot was horribly evident, bulbous and pulsating, stretching the girl into a beach ball.

'She threw up,' said Gabriel. 'Let's go the short way back to the car.'

Diana avoided her husband's face.

*

That night Susan missed supper, but came down for more peppermint tea in front of the TV news, dressed in a voluminous red terrycloth frock like a tent, knot covered.

The screen blinked in and out: another war somewhere. An explosion. Crying brown faces. Marches. Diana thought there were so many more marches these days, so many cross and yelling people. Gabriel and Susan curled on the couch; she didn't understand why they couldn't peel themselves away from each other for a moment. Was that too much to ask?

As they were clearing away tea cups and shattered brandy snaps, the couple told Diana and Jonathan a story.

*

They were coming home one afternoon, to the estate where Susan shared a flat with two old friends. As they rounded the corner of an apartment block, they saw a cluster of humans on the lip of the estate, at least eight tall humans, shadows making them longer, standing in front of a police van. The cluster was quivering, as if an electric current was passing through it, and Gabriel and Susan looked at each other, confused, unsure of what they were seeing.

The cluster broke open, like a strange cocoon. A small boy of about eleven burst through, pulling a bike with him, bits of cop-laughter like soft tendrils stuck to his bike handles and wheels and head. Gabriel took out his phone, aware that his hands were vibrating.

The boy walked rapidly towards another block, pulling keys out of his pocket, talking to himself under his breath, dragging his bike behind him like a heart, and they could see he was shaking too. He ran up the steps and along the first floor, dragging and trembling. They watched him try to fit his key into the door. Gabriel said he looked back and there was but one police officer left; the rest had piled into the van as in a joke skit on an old TV show, and he didn't know why that was so terrifying. The remaining policeman smiled at him and nodded at the phone at his hand as if to say, *Go on then, son. What will you do?*

Gabriel turned back to see Susan walking away from him and towards the boy, stretching her long, dark limbs out, calling, 'Hey, hey, you there, boy, hey,' but the kid couldn't hear her over his own shaking keys. She came to a stop under his block, calling, willing him to hear her, almost singing, so gentle, *hey you, hey you, hey you,* like an amen, and time slowed down to a soft and creeping thing, and the boy eventually looked up.

'You OK?' said Susan.

'They always stop me,' said the boy. 'They always stop me.'

'Hey,' murmured Susan. 'I see you. I see you. Hey.'

They stayed in that position for a while, Gabriel watching child and woman, her arms outstretched.

*

Diana put a hand to her mouth. Her head pounded; her eyes felt wide and staring, as if she might not be able to close them even if she wanted to, as if she might not sleep again, or read again, or rest, thinking of her son's flesh, and the young boy's flesh, and sending her child into the world. Away from here, where they had always nestled.

She watched Gabriel's hand, patting and rubbing the throbbing horror of Susan's belly; his other hand laid peaceful on his young, flat stomach. Watched the young woman's fingers, up and down and around his brown wrists, like playing a musical instrument.

*

The last morning of the visit, Diana was woken by the knot, rubbing itself against her bedroom door and whimpering. She got up, pulled on jeans and boots, clicked her tongue softly at the expanding, quivering ball. It sat wedged in her hallway, fluffy sides brushing against the walls. Flesh bared through wool, moulting. She couldn't imagine how Susan accommodated its mass.

'Come boy, come.'

It trailed behind her, panting.

On the rich, fishy bank, she bent to pet it among the worms, rubbing her fingers around the knot's beaded, antediluvian eyes. It smelled like coconut water, such a delicate aroma, but as she touched it, the smell changed and became more pungent.

She must be quick, she must be sure.

She fed the knot three of her favourite books, tearing the pages out and saving the hardback covers for last. She fed it a set of yellow cotton bedsheets she'd bought last summer. She fed it a lamp from the study she'd never cared for and then she lifted the knot in her arms, cooing and clucking, its breath hot on her shoulder, and used all her strength to throw it into the river.

The knot thrashed, squealed, sucked in water, sank.

Diana sat on the bank and watched the ducks. People out walking dogs. Greyhounds were fashionable this year. Dachshunds pulled too hard on the lead. A Dalmatian would be pretentious. Another Bichon would make her sad.

At home, she told Jonathan it was time for another dog now, please.

When it came to say goodbye, she found she could step forward to press her forehead against the young girl's own, to breathe, for a moment, the same cold air.

Dawn Visited

after Rita Dove

Richard Georges

If I never felt the brush
of a trushie's wing: his pearly-eyed
stare, his feathered splendour
sings where a tree no longer stands.
If I don't look again

at the scars in this earth,
at my stigmata skin,
at the golden guava broken —
its blood will sugar sweet
the greening blades. We know

the future forever happens.
The book is open — this whole world
is yours to imagine! All I know is
it won't if you don't rise to see —
to meet alive the firing sky.

The Apocrypha of O

Gaele Sobott

Fine ash twists through O's locks, settles on her eyelashes and mixes with the dewy perspiration on her skin to form a clay-like paste. She has stained her lips and eyelids purple with blackberry dye; a proud member of the coastal Firefly Squad, a warrior seed collector waging war against the extinction of species. Her boots still hold together, stitched and glued and resoled by old Dinkum, who used to be a cobbler such a very long time ago. She leans on a crutch of ornate wrought iron, crafted from the molten remains of the gates of the watchers' compound where she now lives. Her chest rises and falls with the effort of travelling crookedly through the blackened husks of trees.

She tightens her buttocks, holds, then releases. Breathes out. Flexes her pelvic floor muscles like she is sitting on a grape and lifting it slowly up her vagina. She lets go and treads soft as a smoky mouse scampering across the ashen earth. Her eyes flit from hollows in the ground to burnt-out tree trunks, searching. She listens, disquieted by the absence of birdsong, no symphonies of frogs, no cicadas.

Gravelly voices from her collection of books resonate in the quiet, in her skull.

The world shall be turned into the old silence seven days ... no man shall remain.

A ragged mouthful of the stench of rotting flesh turns her stomach. Behind a fallen tree, she finds scorched fur, a kangaroo, his arms curled in submission, burnt to bone. Maggots squirm thick from within his guts. O stumbles; her left hand grabs hold of a *Eucalyptus globoidea*. The trunk stops her fall, her heat beating against the stringy bark, its scorched hardwood intact, strong for now.

The land … shall be waste and untrodden, and men shall see it desolate … the days are coming when those who dwell on earth shall be seized with great terror … There shall be chaos also in many places, and fire shall often break out…

Seed pouches sway around her hips, attached by clips to her belt. Japanese prints with white cranes on a black background, traditional indigo *sashiko*, Dutch prints from Africa; some are the faded colours of old saris. She guards her fabrics as jealously as she guards her books in her underground home. Her valuables collected during the days when women from around the world stood in solidarity with their struggle. Before nations turned inwards in fits of shrivelling paranoia. Before the watchers escaped to their new settlements on Mars. No spaceships now. No planes. No ships, just small boats that brave the angry seas.

O sews her pouches by hand; small, fine stitches, close together. She lines each pouch with pastel silk.

Her breathing evens, she stretches her arms, looks up at the dirty sky and at the headless testament to a tree against which she leans, canopies burnt to nothing, top kill. These trees have little chance of epicormic recovery. She bends her head, eyes wandering the ground. Wedged under a blackened root lie gumnuts.

'I see you, I see you little ones,' she croons in low song, shaking some red-brown seeds into one of her pouches. She bends to lay the pods back down under the root on fertile cinders. 'I sing rain for you. I dance rain for you.'

And the earth shall restore those that are asleep in her, and so shall the dust those that dwell in silence, and the secret places shall deliver those souls that were committed unto them.

A tree cracks like a stock whip and crashes down somewhere not too far away. Trees, bone-dry from consecutive winters with little to no rain, topple, no warning, weakened by one fire after another.

And they shall break down the cities and walls, mountains and hills, trees of the wood, and grass of the meadows…

Something, someone, walks with heavy stride. O grabs her crutch and moves behind a large log, lays flat, rolls her brown arms in ash slowly, until they are the grey of the earth. A rogue watcher who stinks of sour skin, unwashed, stomps up to the kangaroo, hacking, sucking. Probably the tail. Maybe the maggots. O unsheathes a blade. The watcher mumbles and the forest is quiet again for an instant. So close.

A voice speaks smooth and strong like thick treacle in O's brain.

The angel ... waiteth with a sword to cut thee in two, and to destroy you.

O thinks, *I am that angel, I will cut the enemy in two*, trying to concentrate, straining now to listen to the watcher.

Metal jabs cold and hard against the back of her head, her mouth and tongue are gritty with dirt, her lip splits, front tooth smashes against wood where there is a pleasant scent of burnt resin.

I saw Trees of Judgement, especially vessels of the fragrance of incense and myrrh ... I saw seven mountains full of fine nard, and fragrant trees of cinnamon and pepper...

Her mouth tastes of iron, blood.

'You're a scrawny little crip fuck but you'll taste better than a festering fucking roo,' the watcher snarls.

O can't see her, but realises by her voice and her way of talking that she and the watcher are probably about the same age. Most of the watchers bought tickets on the space shuttles. Adapt, they said, and paid for expensive fireproof houses for themselves and helicopter ships and underground compounds, and they plundered the earth and the rivers and the skies without mercy. Adapt. Of those who stayed, few survived. A few rogues remain. This was surely one.

A trigger clicks; everything is moving, changing. A war cry, guttural but so loud the charcoaled trees shudder. Explosion.

O opens one eye to see blood trickling down the log. She doesn't feel any pain. Maybe she is an angel. A hand grabs her arm. O shrieks as she is pulled up onto her feet.

Millendevoe stands, muscled, dark, oiled skin, their black hair braided into a sculptured circle that stands upright at the back of their head. Tattooed circles on the left side of their face. A Revolutionary Malo Kingi, small and lethal.

And another voice from another book whispers.

A cold sweat covers me/ trembling seizes my body/ and I am greener than grass. Lacking but little of death do I seem.

Millendevoe holds O's arm too tight, glaring at her, 'Read my lips! Fireflies must always go out in pairs, twos, one plus one. A partner to keep an eye out for danger. There is a reason for the rule, yeah?'

They shove O's head so she's facing the watcher's body. 'A reason, right?'

O is surprised at how much the watcher looks just like her, same golden-brown skin, same kind of lanky. Full lips, green eyes. But her hair's been cut short to the scalp, she's filthy and there's an ugly hole in her chest.

'How did you know I left the compound alone?' O asks.

'Dinkum told me,' Millendevoe says, handing O her crutch.

O bends over the watcher. Her hand touches the woman's breast, the thin cotton T-shirt warm beneath her fingers, down the curve of her hip, delving into pockets. She produces a pocket knife, a pen and a green stone. She holds the stone up to the sun and seems to be imbibing the colour.

'New-leaf green, the green we need to see in our forests.' The corners of her mouth lift slightly to suggest a smile, her cheeks are plump, round.

'It's a healing gem, calming,' she says lightly, touching the stone to Millendevoe's lips. 'A stone of unconditional love. You feel it?'

Millendevoe is still and silent. Their face expressionless. Their black eyes focused on O's.

'The colour matches your eyes,' they finally say.

O takes a deep breath. She puts the stone into one of her seed pouches and the pen in her pocket.

Millendevoe asks, 'You're a writer, yeah?'

'I write.'

'Do you publish?'

'The city isn't interested in erotic fantasy.'

'Oh?' They raise their eyebrows, small crinkles appear on their brow.

'I print my stories and I sew fabric covers and I bind them with colourful thread. People buy from me or barter. I'll show you sometime.'

O fiddles with the pocket knife, unclips a rubber bottle from her belt and squeezes sanitiser over the various little tools, a screwdriver, a bottle opener, the knife. She holds the small blade against the top of Millendevoe's arm, just where it begins to curve into their shoulder.

'Do you think it's sharp?'

'I don't know. Why don't you test it?'

O tilts the blade and presses. 'You sure?'

They nod.

She draws a fine line of blood about three centimetres long. Millendevoe doesn't flinch.

'It's sharp,' O says, running her hand around Millendevoe's belt, across the handle of their rifle and over the handcuffs, stepping closer and pressing against their padded vest.

Then beautiful swift sparrows led you over the black earth/ from the sky through the middle air/ whirling their wings into a blur.

Millendevoe pulls away. They pick up the watcher's gun.

'This is high-tech. You could take out a spy drone with this. A sniper's dream come true.'

'No more drones, no more surveillance, no Eye in the Sky, their gutless army is gone. We're okay. Don't need that weapon,' O replies.

'It's still useful. Listen, I'm escorting you back to the compound. I got stuff to do.'

'Stuff?' O asks.

'Firstly, I need to organise a team to dispose of these two bodies.'

'Bury the kangaroo?'

'Burn it, probably. Biosecurity.'

'Good earth, no!' O's mouth contorts in disdain, 'Leave these bones, the spirit, on Country. It'll provide nutrients to the soil for years. I'll report it to Umbarra research centre. They'll assess any risk.'

'Is that where you take your seeds?'

'Yeah, me and four other Fireflies work with the reseeding programme. They trained us. Blakfulla science. Latin names are like dead beetles pinned in rows. We're just beginning the learning of how each plant and animal and insect and the rain and wind and stars are interdependent, the cycles...'

'You're lucky to get in. That place is one of the best.'

'They're the best in plant-based medicines. Developed Globoidnan A for HIV and an effective vaccine against SARS-CoV-2.'

'Okay, tell your work about the roo. I'll deal with the dead watcher and I need to get a couple of MK comrades to comb the area for rogues, find where she was hiding, maybe more weapons, ammunition caches. Let's go.'

O holds Millendevoe at the elbow. This way she is steadier and can walk faster.

'Are you Yuin?' Millendevoe asks.

'Not by birth, Dad was from Brazil, Mum's from Poland, but I'm a proud citizen of Yuin Country.'

They walk in the quiet of the burnt bush. No birdsong, no symphonies of frogs, no cicadas. O listens to Millendevoe swallow. Her fingers are super-sensitive to the smooth skin of Millendevoe's inner arm, the veins, the arteries, the pulsing blood. Their footsteps beat a rhythmic accompaniment.

She says ten thousand times: To walk a hundred steps with one another,/ Is enough to develop a lingering affinity.

At the compound, Dinkum shuffles towards them. He gives O a coil of thin brown leather cord. 'I thought you might have some use for this,' he says.

O smiles. 'Thank you, Uncle.'

Millendevoe makes a move to leave. They pat O twice on the back. 'Fireflies must always go out in pairs. That's the rule, yeah?'

'Are you going to report me?' O asks.

'Don't know. I got to give it some thought. Individualism, the greater good, that kind of thing.'

O heads over to the canteen. She eats potato salad and greens and a big bowl of red jelly, stewed pears and custard.

Her bunker is set into a hill, no stairs, even access all the way through. Plenty of light from the sun tunnels. It's small: a bathroom, bedroom/lounge and tiny kitchen space. Books line the walls and are scattered on every surface. Her bound works are piled up in bright colours on a book shelf near the door. A typewriter and laptop sit among fabrics and sewing materials on a desk built into an alcove. She peels off her clothes, shoves them into the washing machine, steps into the shower and blasts hot water over her breasts, her head, her face. She washes the ash and blood and blackberry dye from her face, scrubs her dirty arms, cleans her teeth, then stands for a while, allowing the hot water to pummel her back.

Body blushing, red, hot, swollen, she holds the handrail and steps out onto the bath mat. Towel-dries her hair and ties it, still damp, into a knot on the top of her head; a thin lock escapes and falls loose against her neck. She dresses in a faux-leather, open-nipple bra and harness, which circles her neck like a choker and buckles at the back. Pulls a black, shiny, fishnet tube with wide diamond gaps up past her thighs around her buttocks and stretches it across her pelvis, the fleshy mound above her vulva *au naturel*, unwaxed, unshaved. Her belt is slung low around her hips, the pocket knife, tools, toys attached. She paints her lips and eyelids with blackberry dye and drags a fishnet mask down over her hair, spreading it over her eyes, her mouth, her face. She polishes her boots with emu oil so they shine, then ties the laces around her thin ankles.

An electric-green strap-on, a supersex pleasure-giver, hangs on her bedpost, spilling psychedelic green light into the room. She mixes oil from the cinnamon-smelling bark of Acacia leprosa *with oil from the brown flowers of* Boronia megastigma. *Parts her legs, tips her head back, her fingers searching, clammy, overwhelmed by the complex scent, soft and floral at first, then spicy verging on wood...*

The door opens. Millendevoe steps in framed by the purple evening sky. They stand close to O and hand her a pair of handcuffs and a small leather flogger with ten tails.

'Let's take this slow and slinky, yeah. Set the scene, tell me one of your stories.'

Notes

In order of appearance, the voices that speak to O are from:
2 Esdras 7:30
2 Esdras 5:3-8
2 Esdras 7:32
2 Esdras 7:32
2 Esdras 15:43
Susanna 1:59
Enoch 26:1
Poems of Sappho
Poems of Sappho
The Plum in the Golden Vase by Jin Ping Mei
The Apocrypha of O

VII yesterday/today

'we ran a gay story last week'

A Stranger Here Myself

Paul Burston

I knew I wasn't quite right from an early age. My mother knew, but did the best she could. The other kids knew and tried to beat it out of me. They failed.

As a small boy in small-town south Wales, I never learned how to fit in. I was always the last to be picked for team sports, the first to be singled out as gay, the last to defend myself when cornered in the playground or at the school gate. I was the boy who didn't fight back. Not then. Not like that.

As a teenager, I stopped trying to blend in and began to embody what queer theorists call 'cultures of resistance'. In other words, I wore my queerness like armour, experimenting with outlandish clothes, hair dye and makeup. But it was the early 1980s. Gender-bending was all the rage. My effeminate appearance had unexpected consequences. It attracted girlfriends. Suddenly, I was both standing out and fitting in — and still not out of the closet.

My mother wasn't fooled. To her, my appearance was proof that I wasn't 'quite right in the head.' The same applied to my sense of humour. 'A good joke would kill you!' she'd say as I roared with laughter at Kenny Everett or – horror of horrors! – *Spitting Image*.

Despite my academic achievements – I was the first person in my family to go to university – this feeling of being not quite right never left me. And that was before I finally came out as gay and faced the rejection many young LGBTQ+ people experience from their own families.

I grew up in a house without books, in which homosexuality was only ever mentioned as the butt of jokes on TV or the subject of some scandal in the tabloid newspapers my stepdad read at the breakfast table. There were no gay characters on soap operas when I was a child, no *Beautiful Thing*, no *Queer as Folk*, no *Glee* and certainly no social media to connect me with like-minded people and assure me that I wasn't alone.

Cruelly, the sense of isolation you feel as a young LGBTQ+ person is often magnified by those closest to you. You're a stranger to yourself and to your own family. Growing up in a predominantly white, working-class community, two of my school friends were a young boy from Uganda and a lad whose father came from Iraq. Both boys experienced racism at school. But neither feared going home to their parents and explaining why they were being bullied. When I was bullied, I kept it to myself.

Unless you're one of the lucky ones, LGBTQ+ people grow up fearing that, as soon as your parents discover you're different, they'll reject you. I certainly did. So you try to hide who you are. You repress your feelings and shroud your sexuality in shame. This causes psychological damage. Your sense of otherness festers and grows. Some people never fully recover from it, but become self-loathing, self-harming, self-medicating or suicidal. Like many gay teenagers, I contemplated suicide. I self-medicated for years. Internalised homophobia is something I've worked hard to overcome.

This is my lived experience, and the experience of many other LGBTQ+ people. This is where we're coming from. We know what exclusion feels like. We're familiar with the ways in which words can be used as weapons — and the wounds they can inflict. We know that people don't always say what they mean, or mean what they say. So when someone says 'you're not quite right for us', we interpret these words through years of alienation, otherness and rejection.

When I was growing up, a popular euphemism for being gay was 'one of *them*', as in, 'No, he hasn't got a girlfriend. He's one of *them*!' The words were whispered in hushed tones, with an emphasis on 'them' to indicate how strange and distasteful such people were. So if people like me are 'them', then who are 'we'? Can this division be breached? Can 'one of them' ever truly become 'one of us'?

Exclusion isn't always explicit. The words aren't always said directly. In the same way many white people are unaware of or defensive about the idea of white privilege, many heterosexuals are unaware or defensive about the notion of straight privilege. I still hear well-meaning heterosexuals suggest that 'it's easy to be gay now' — as if homophobia somehow ceased to exist when legal equality was achieved, making it safe for me to walk the street hand in hand with my same-sex partner. If only this were true — but it so often isn't, even now, even in a big city like London. People like me don't take public space for granted. We know it's not always safe out there. We've got the message. We've had it punched and kicked into us.

The writer and AIDS activist Larry Kramer once said that straight liberals were gay people's worst enemy, because they helped maintain the illusion of tolerance. I disagree. In my opinion, we need all the allies we can find. But they need to be willing to do the work. It shouldn't be left to LGBTQ+ people to educate and explain ourselves all the time, any more than it should be left to black people to talk to white people about race. Tolerance isn't the same as acceptance — and acceptance isn't the same as inclusion. All too often, it leads to tokenism.

Here's an example. A gay male friend on a national newspaper once attended an editorial meeting and suggested they run a piece about a reported rise in homophobic hate crimes. His suggestion was rejected on the grounds that 'we ran a gay story last week.' The story they had run the previous week was an interview with the singer Boy George. The message was loud and clear: some gay stories were acceptable, others weren't suitable for a national newspaper. This is tokenism, plain and simple.

I've been a journalist for thirty years and an author for almost as long. Back in 2007, I published my third novel with a mainstream publisher. Before writing fiction, I'd published several non-fiction books, including an academic anthology about queerness and popular culture, a pop biography and a book of travel writing. I was twelve years into my career as a published author but, in all that time, I'd never once been invited to take part in a book festival.

Now that I'm working on my seventh novel and have also edited two short story collections, I've had plenty of time to think about why this might be. It seems to me that gay fiction is acceptable to the people who make these decisions, provided it's deemed to be 'literary' enough. But who decides what is and isn't 'literary'? And why should LGBTQ+ writers be obliged to write in any given style? Our lives, experiences, methods of storytelling and styles of writing are as varied and as valid as anyone else's.

Comic fiction is often sniffed at, despite the fact that comedy can have just as much to tell us about the human condition as any other genre. Of course, I would say that; my first four novels were all classed as comedies of manners, though the vein of humour running through them grew darker and darker until finally I realised that, inside this writer of comic fiction, there was a different kind of novelist struggling to get out. So a few years ago, I moved to the dark side and began writing crime, another genre often regarded as disreputable.

Sometimes it isn't homophobia or even heterosexism you're up against, but just plain old snobbery. I once took part in a books podcast for a national newspaper. At one point, the interviewer turned to me and said, rather witheringly: 'And you write those books with the glittery covers.' I asked her if she'd read any of them. It quickly became clear that she hadn't.

It was out of this frustration that I launched the Polari literary salon in 2007. Polari is a live showcase for LGBTQ+ writers of all descriptions, at any stage of their career. It began small, in the upstairs room of a bar in Soho, and grew quickly, moving to two other West End venues before settling in at the Southbank Centre in 2009. We also tour regularly. We've performed in theatres, libraries, arts centres, pubs and nightclubs, and are equally at home in the Royal Festival Hall and the Royal Vauxhall Tavern. We've even performed on a race course.

From the outset, I had a very clear idea of what Polari should be: accessible, lively, inclusive. I also had a strong sense of what it shouldn't be: dry, solemn, exclusive. With apologies to Oscar Wilde, I pity any poor man or woman trapped at an author event where everyone is self-important and over-earnest. Literary events can and should be fun. Laughter needn't denote a lack of seriousness. As Wilde also wrote: 'If you want to tell people the truth, make them laugh, otherwise they'll kill you.'

At the risk of killing my chances of ever being invited to a book festival again, the truth is that far too many of them fall into the same trap, whereby authors and audiences alike are drawn from the same narrow social demographic. I wanted Polari to embrace everyone: writers of all ages, races and genders, from all classes and cultural backgrounds, working in a wide variety of genres. There's no point in creating a live literary platform in the name of diversity if it doesn't reflect the diversity within the communities it's supposed to represent.

When I programme my events, I do my best to ensure that the line-ups are as diverse as possible. I don't only do this because I think it's the right thing to do; I do it because it makes for a far better audience experience. People like to see themselves reflected on stage — and why shouldn't they? I've attended literary events where there is no LGBTQ+ representation at all, or perhaps one white gay man or woman invited to speak on behalf of us all. I've attended others where there's been one woman on a panel with four men, or one person of colour on an otherwise all-white platform. What this says to me is that some people are still 'not quite right for us', and that some attempts at inclusion don't go nearly far enough.

Part of Polari's remit is to encourage and nurture new talent. Over the years we've hosted some extraordinarily gifted writers, many of whom are just starting out and have never read their work in public before. We offer them a supportive space in which to showcase their work, alongside some of the biggest names in the LGBTQ+ literary world.

So it seemed only natural that in 2011 we launched the Polari First Book Prize for new LGBTQ+ writing. The prize is open to writers born or based in the UK and Ireland, whose first book explores LGBTQ+ themes. All kinds of books are eligible, from debut novels to volumes of poetry, fiction and non-fiction, memoirs, graphic novels and more. We've had a wide range of winners: memoirist James Maker; poet John McCullough; novelists Saleem Haddad, Paul McVeigh and Fiona Mozley; crime writer Mari Hannah; short-story writers Kirsty Logan and Diriye Osman. In 2019, we added a second Polari Book Prize for non-debuts, which was won by poet Andrew McMillan. In 2020, the prizes were won by Amrou Al-Kadhi and Kate Davies.

The number of submissions has risen year on year, and more than doubled in the last year alone. The quality of entries is strong and ever more diverse. We've enjoyed support from WHSMITH TRAVEL, which showcases the shortlisted books, and from a wide variety of media outlets, from *The Bookseller* to Out News Global to the *Times of India*.

And yet. Eleven years after launching the Polari First Book Prize – still the UK's only book award for LGBTQ+ writing – we're unable to attract a major corporate sponsor, relying instead on the generosity of our PR company FMcM Associates and my agent at DHH Literary Agency to provide prize money. The prize itself is run entirely voluntarily and involves an ever-increasing amount of work. This can't be right. Surely the UK's only book prize dedicated to LGBTQ+ writing is worth more than this? Or are we still not significant enough for the corporations regularly awarded prizes for their commitment to equality, diversity and inclusion?

I realise, of course, that as soon as you run your own literary salon and create a book prize, you've automatically become one of the gatekeepers in some people's minds. No longer 'them', now 'us'. Maybe there's some truth in this. All I can say is that the prize has an independent panel of judges and that I'm every bit as dedicated to supporting new talent now as I was fourteen years ago when Polari first began.

In many ways, I'm still a stranger here myself. The worlds of journalism and publishing are both far more middle class now than they were when I first started out. Yet, despite running my own literary salon, founding a book prize, publishing over a dozen books and thousands of newspaper and magazine articles and reviews, I have never been invited to judge any other book prize. Not once. Why not? I wish I knew.

Maybe the time will come when there are no gatekeepers, no 'us' and 'them', when we're all equal and have the same opportunities and nobody is made to feel as if they're 'not quite right'. Until then, I'll continue as I am. One of them. One of us. Doing what I can and hoping it makes a difference.

My Communist Friend

– for Walter Famler

John Mateer

Later, in Vienna, my friend the Communist would tell me of his own lost love, how he had followed her to Istanbul only to find out that she was from one of *those* families, daughter of a millionaire. He had tried to be an agitator there, was involved with the Kurdistan Workers' Party up in the mountains, travelled with a pistol in his rucksack. Years later, when he returned to Istanbul for a conference, she agreed to meet and picked him up from his hotel in her limousine. His colleagues were impressed: *He'd been the lover of the woman now president of Turkey's Chamber of Commerce!* When they'd broken up, he had tried to join a Sufi monastery. My friend the Communist believes his life could have been very different. He could have been a millionaire.

'Maybe you should try the Sufis again?'

'I can't. Once refused, always refused.'

Sisyphus, deformed, looks back over his shoulder

Andy Jackson

The hill is everywhere beyond my front door
    and what I carry can never be put down.

      It's hard to remember a time when this
    weight was separate from my body. Aware

        it's being watched, the skin grows quickly
          over a burden, hardens like a myth,

          but keeps its sensitivity. There's a constant
          hum in my inner ear, and my nervous

          system is awash with fatigue. The enduring
          task is to leave the house, practise the art of

      oblivion, as if that could deflect your attention.
      At least it's exercise. Or rehearsal. For what,

      I'm not sure. Am I lifting history? Your
    thoughts of me? The hill could be the entire

      human world. The hill could be my shame,
    steadfast and cumbersome. Each morning,

I wake spent, begin again – scale and descend,
    scale and descend, the steep face of my

      appearance. Who else clambers up this
    fateful inclination, assumes this otherness?

At the summit, breathless, alone, all I
can do now is take it in – the vertiginous

outlook I never asked for. I have left these
impressions in the earth. I will be followed.

A Cruel Nakedness

E. Ethelbert Miller

When money was just as good as cash
we sat by the curb and shook our cups.
We held signs against our chests.

Signs with words no one took time to read.
It was as if we were writers hanged upside down
after a revolution.

Our bodies twisting between the earth
and sky as if the old order of things
could once again survive or take flight.

A few coins placed in a hand
become the first line of a prayer.
A glance or hello is a hymn of salvation.

But each day we fail to return kindness
to the world. Strangers pass strangers
afraid of blood or bond.

There is a cruel nakedness among people
that is already visible to the touch.
How alone we live before we die.

'I'm quite alright with that'

Olive Senior

'Not quite right for us.' I have encountered these words many times in the publishing world, where they are usually tossed around, but they haven't left much of a mark on me. I have come to conflate this phrase with another – 'This just won't do' – both spoken by a particular kind of gatekeeper and, for me since childhood, both forming the pivot on which resistance turns. Yet I had no idea how deeply entrenched this resistance is in me until I started to think about the phrase. This led me to see how many times in my poetry and fiction my speakers have resisted both these notions; without conscious thought, I'd like to say, on the part of the writer.

First to come to mind is the woman in the poem 'Hurricane Story 1951': the migrant aspirant nurse who ends up stuck swabbing the floors in an English hospital and who keeps pouring out more and more water from her pail to create the metaphorical ocean that will reunite her with her long-lost son in Jamaica. Her resounding 'No!' to Matron's 'Miss Black, this just won't do' embodies a larger shout out against all the injustice and racism she has faced since a hurricane blew her away from her island. This England that, in 1951, was approached as the Promised Land, the Mother Country for the *Windrush* generation, with a protective Mother, Missis Queen. What the emigrants encountered instead were white gatekeepers everywhere saying, 'Your presence just won't do.'

In my childhood, I never understood the source of the common saying, 'If you go to England, you bound to turn mad', even though there were several embodiments of this notion roaming around our rural district. Later, in my Kingston neighbourhood, I would observe a man passing my house each day who was clearly one of those that England had 'turned mad', from the way he dressed and carried himself, walking like an automaton. Years later, he morphed into the Uncle in 'The Case Against the Queen', who apologises for bombarding HM with letters requesting her intervention to receive an apology and compensation for being incarcerated in English hospitals, where they effected 'indignity' on his person, taking out his heart and replacing it with a mechanical contrivance. I can hear him throwing back at the gatekeepers 'This just won't do' in his newly acquired English accent (though he doesn't actually use those words); his packet of crumbling, unsent letters in a trunk and the embarrassment of his madness the only legacies he will leave family from his lengthy sojourn in that land of opportunity.

My 'mad woman' in 'You Think I Mad, Miss?' is not into apology; she simply asserts her right to tell her story to motorists trapped by the red light at a busy city intersection, whether or not they want to hear. Embedded in her fragmented autobiography is her resistance to authority figures: her mother; a psychiatrist at the mental hospital; and the schoolteacher from her youth who instigated her supposed 'fall'.

Children of Empire who are taught to read and write love to employ Massa's tools against him. The adult protesters – Uncle or the 'Mad Woman' – all proudly assert their literary skills and their right to use them against oppression. 'Ever see me without my paper and pencil yet? Ever see me without my shoes and stocking and two slip under my dress?' Isabella Francina Myrtella Jones demands of her listeners, conflating the literacy and pseudo-respectability she has been taught. The narrator of my novel *Dancing Lessons*, though lacking a high school education, gains words, wisdom and erudition over a lonely life filled with reading, and employs the writing of a journal (which becomes the book) as a way of untangling a lifetime of embarrassing missteps. Writing finally enables her to reclaim a true-true self initially scarred by the denigration of her black ancestry by her white family members; the shame of her mentally ill father and out-of-wedlock mother, who had the temerity to die in childbirth, forever marking the unwanted orphan foisted on them as 'not quite right for us'.

Although in these and other works I am clearly fascinated by outsiders, the challengers of authority, and the way they affirm their humanity, not all of them can be labelled insane or unwanted. Many are those other outsiders: children. Their resistance takes the same form as that of the adults, as they ignore the 'rules' and simply speak — in literary terms, sidestepping publishing's low-impact rejection of 'not quite right for us' by going directly into self-publishing. Children also recognise the power of the book and what is embodied in the written word, and early in life find ways to use this to enforce their own passive resistance. (In my own childhood, I recognised that having your head buried in a book was a way of getting adults to leave you alone, as that marked you as the child 'not giving trouble'.)

In my story 'Confirmation Day', the child emerging from the church realises that the religious ceremony in which the elders in her family have placed so much store to make her a Child of God has not, in fact, changed her one bit. Gazing at a cloud-free sky, she is shocked to discover 'a new-found power' in herself and that nothing can conquer her, not the Communion wine she has just taken, nor *The Book of Common Prayer*. She will no doubt go on to write her own book.

The little girl in 'Do Angels Wear Brassieres?' literally throws the book at authority. She is studying the Bible in secret, not from conviction, but to find ways of besting hypocritical adults. Her respectable aunt's tea party and the visiting Archdeacon's dignity both come crashing down through her audacity, in first asking the clergyman trick questions to test his Bible knowledge and then, finally, 'Do angels wear brassieres?'

One of my first published adult stories, a novella titled *Ballad*, reflects this same assertion of personhood, of the right to speak even when there is an effort to silence. At the behest of her teacher (no doubt a *Reader's Digest* reader), an eleven-year-old country girl writes a composition about 'The Most Unforgettable Character I Ever Meet'. In a rural Jamaican version of 'not quite right for us', Teacher promptly rips up the pages because she feels the subject, a reputedly sexually loose village woman, is 'not fit person to write a composition about'. Does this give the child pause? Hardly. She decides to tell the story of her friend directly to the world, at first wanting to use the only literary model she thinks suitable for a tale of love and death: the English ballad. But then she decides she can't sing and that 'this whole thing too deep and wide for a little thing like a ballad'. Untutored in method, she manages to evade censorship and use her mouth. 'I will just tell you the story,' she says, and broadcasts it to the world.

People frequently ask me if I am the child in these stories and of course I deny it, as I believe all writers should deny any connection with their characters. But I am now at an age where I can confess that, while the characters are not me and the stories are not mine, they certainly embody my own lifelong impulse to subvert authority, to challenge fake respectability, to shrug off the gatekeepers of personhood, history and story. This is what has enabled me to endure a lifetime of writing and publishing on my own terms, my usual mental response to 'not quite right for us' being a resounding: 'No. It is not.' This started with requests to rewrite the Jamaican creole in my first story collection, *Summer Lightning*, in Standard English to make it 'suitable'. (Finally published without changes by Longman, *Summer Lightning* went on to win the first Commonwealth Writers Prize.)

It is the 'quite' in that phrase that annoys me, as does the 'suit' in the similar 'this just won't suit'. 'Quite' seems the sort of word that would be used only by certain people, implying as it does queueing, quality, qualifications, inquisition — and the Q for the quiet sign warning you that, in this hallowed place, you are a barefoot mendicant among the besuited. 'Quite' is gatekeeper doublespeak with a sneer that is absent from the straightforward 'not right for us', spoken with a particular plummy accent, one that has silenced me since childhood; a polished accent of belonging that goes with the perfect place setting. I can honestly say I have never wanted to sit in that place. Even without the accent, 'not quite right' and 'this won't suit' or 'this just won't do' emanated from people who endorsed certain conservative expectations – especially of girl children at the time I was growing up – and the attributes that they valued, all outward expressions of conformity.

Only much later, in adulthood, have I realised how 'suit' is the operative word for the environment I grew up in, one in which appearance trounced substance, where outward 'respectability' masked inner hunger or wicked desires in the rush to be the good colonial subject. Where children were groomed and socialised to be 'right' and 'ripe' for the world that awaited, one that imposed a false identity that had nothing to do with us, as I noted in my poem 'Colonial Girls School', since it 'Told us nothing about ourselves/There was nothing about us at all'.

This poem upset at least one former principal of my girls' school and some of my peers, who see it as slander on that excellent institution, but they missed the point entirely. I was writing about not one but *all* our schools, girls' and boys', and the curriculum at the time, which was that of English grammar schools. I have said often that I am thankful for the excellent education and the rigorous intellectual grounding that I and people of my generation received from these schools. The critique is not of what was there, but of what was missing; forcing us to fit into a suit that was not quite right for us because of, let us say, the poor sizing, the lack of detailing, wrong or missing buttons, sewn-up pockets, perhaps the unsuitable colour or threadbare finish.

'Colonial Girls School' remains one of my most popular poems. What is sad is that, although it was written so long ago, when I've had the temerity to say to schoolgirls today, 'I was writing about my time; I'm glad that for you things have changed' (with a Caribbean-oriented curriculum, among other things), they quite often assure me, 'Nothing has changed, Miss.'

A lot *has* changed in our post-independence Caribbean and in our schools, but 'nothing has changed' in our inability to cast off the deep-seated colonial trappings that still reinforce value in the metaphorical suit over the healthy development of the inner life: suit as straitjacket. Mental slavery now is underscored by a new form of colonisation; witness the widespread influence of American Christian fundamentalist religion (which, for instance, in some schools, is placing girls in ankle-length uniforms, inches longer than those we had to wear generations ago in our colonial girls' school). My poem, though, ends on an optimistic note:

> For isn't it strange how
> northern eyes
> in the brighter world before us now
>
> Pale?

'Pale northern eyes' is referenced earlier in the poem:

> How those pale northern eyes and
> aristocratic whispers once erased us
> How our loudness, our laughter
> debased us

As a child growing up in a world of mainly dark-eyed people, I genuinely associated 'pale northern eyes' with the Other — though in retrospect, it cannot be the eyes alone, but what they represented, since my father and most of my siblings have light-coloured eyes. But the fading influence of the iconic 'northern eyes' marked our emergence into self, my peers and I, as we stepped out into the world. That was true of those of us who hadn't entirely bought into wearing the metaphorical suit, anyway; many did.

Since early childhood, I've known that I would be an artist, though what kind and how remained elusive, since I had no mentors or guides. In a way, this has suited me, for it enabled me to pursue my own erratic, bumbling, eccentric, sometimes painful but independent path, one in which 'not quite right for us' can be easily deflected, because there are so many paths to self-expression and self-affirmation. I am fully aware that this is not the path for everyone, nor am I advocating it — especially in today's world, where art is more than ever dominated by commercial considerations. Each of us has to decide which path we want to pursue.

I like to think, though, that writers are wannabe alchemists, those sage magicians seeking to turn dross to gold, a lifelong striving that might end in futility. The gain is always in the process of finding out. So, if you receive a note saying 'not quite right for us', it is not the end; merely the beginning.

Notes

'Hurricane Story 1951', *Gardening in the Tropics*. Toronto: Insomniac Press, 2005, pp. 35–43.

'The Case Against the Queen', *Discerner of Hearts*. Toronto: McClelland and Stewart, 1995, pp. 38–56.

'You Think I Mad, Miss?', *Discerner of Hearts*. Toronto: McClelland and Stewart, 1995, pp. 75–82.

Dancing Lessons. Toronto: Cormorant Press, 2011.

'Confirmation Day', *Summer Lightning*. Harlow: Longman, 1986, pp. 85–99.

'Do Angels Wear Brassieres?', *Summer Lightning*. Harlow: Longman, 1986, pp. 67–79.

'Ballad', *Summer Lightning*. Harlow: Longman, 1986, pp. 100–34.

'Colonial Girls School', *Talking of Trees*. Kingston, JA: Calabash, 1985, pp. 26–7.

VIII today/tomorrow

'Bend our words and the worlds we create to fit?'

The Days the World Stood Still

Nick Makoha

In my lifetime, I've not yet seen an event that has changed the course of history in this way. If this pandemic has highlighted anything, it is that life *matters* — not that morning coffee at PRET A MANGER, or how your stock portfolio is doing, or which book is going to top the bestseller list.

How did it do that? Well, contrary to what the media would have us believe, it does not discriminate according to class, colour, race, sexual orientation or religion. Its ability to kill has got our full attention. It has brought the global economy to a standstill; international sports to its knees. Central business districts are ghost towns; many companies have hit the wall. The city break is gone, social life a thing of the past. You could also say it has toppled a US president. Despite all that, my TV keeps wanting me to buy a new car. The question is, where can I go?

The virus has no interest in political rhetoric. A virus is a replicon, a strand of genetic material, either DNA or RNA, surrounded by a protein coat that reproduces itself. This sequence of events is how the virus survives. (Scientists believe that half of human DNA came from viruses.) This pathogenic organism is not classified as being *alive* in the strictest sense of the word. The unit of life is the cell, that 'small room' – as the word translates – held together by a membrane that allows all the chemical reactions necessary for life to occur (such as respiration) in fluid called cytoplasm. These reactions are triggered by the cell's software, which contains at least one chromosome.

Viruses, however, have no membrane and do not perform metabolism or respire. In fact, their ability to replicate is only possible inside the host of a living cell. In the case of SARS-CoV-2, which causes COVID-19, that host is us. The virus turns our genetic material against us by reprograming the cell's DNA and RNA to reproduce the virus's DNA thousands of times, before repeating the process in new cells. The virus transports itself via 'viral shedding'. That is to say, it releases itself from an infected host via coughing or sneezing. Those coughs and sneezes have become more spine-chilling than guns.

I haven't been into central London since March 2019. My car could do with a wash. For the first time since I've owned it, a tank of petrol has lasted me more than six months. My daily run is the only way I get to see the neighbourhood. My son did not want to go to the park or ride his BMX; he was scared that his asthma would make him a target for the virus. I've stopped listening to TV or radio news every day. I could see how it was affecting my family. They sleep longer, say less at the dinner table and don't laugh as much. My at-home clothes have become my work clothes; the dinner table, my office. Our life, like many others, has come to resemble sci-fi/horror. The centre of town could have been used as the opening scene of *28 Days Later* or *I Am Legend*. This is our new normal.

There have been a few times in my life when the world has stood still. Twice, you could argue, it was a case of the same event repeating itself: the births of my two children. When my daughter was born, I shed my boyish ways. I used to burn through money like fire through a field. There was always something that needed buying, some place I had to be. The world seemed so big and I seemed so small. But the world stopped revolving around me when my daughter came. As I held her in my arms for the first time in the hospital ward, I remember thinking, 'I need to make this world a better place for you.' When I look at pictures of me before her birth, I hardly recognise myself. I'm not talking about the loss of hair. It was something in my eyes. I worry more, but I'm happier. The man I was and the man I am now would not recognise each other if they passed themselves in the street.

My son was almost born in our living room. My wife and I had been up the whole night. When he entered the world, I had the strangest feeling of being complete, like a finished jigsaw puzzle or a solved Rubik's Cube.

Other times when the world stood still for me include watching MTV's premiere of MJ's thirteen-minute film *Thriller* in 1983, and when Barack Obama accepted the Democratic Party nomination for President in 2008, in Grant Park, Chicago. These happy moments lasted for a day; COVID-19, on the other hand, is the Groundhog Day that keeps on giving — and not in a good way.

But, now, with all this time available, with a tankful of petrol and nowhere to go, I've realised that there are *other* recent instants in which the world has stood still. From the moment US football star quarterback Colin Kaepernick stopped standing for the national anthem and lost his job in 2016, to the killing of forty-six-year-old George Floyd by police in 2020, it seems that viruses come in all shapes and sizes to attack black bodies, freezing our lives or causing our deaths.

You might ask why Kaepernick stands out, when National Football League (NFL) census data shows that *seventy per cent* of players are African-American (twenty-eight per cent are white, and four per cent comprise Asian/Pacific Islander and non-white Hispanic). First of all, black quarterbacks are unusual — this position is only filled by seventeen per cent of black players in the NFL. Kaepernick also outruns most defensive backs and linebackers. A second-round draft pick, he played for the San Francisco 49ers for six seasons. In other words, if the NFL were a game of chess, Kaepernick would be a king that can move like a knight *and* a bishop. In 2012, after the 49ers replaced their starting quarterback Alex Smith, Kaepernick led the team to its first Super Bowl appearance since 1994. He took them to within ten yards of winning Super Bowl XLVII, and is one of a handful of quarterbacks to record at least three passing touchdowns and 100 yards rushing in a game.

Kaepernick was living the American Dream, but when he took a knee in the 49ers' third pre-season game in 2016, he stopped being an elite sportsman and became a symbol and target. Because of this, he will probably never be nominated to the US Pro Football Hall of Fame. Since 2016, he has been a free agent. He is being treated similarly to Muhammad Ali, forced into premature retirement at the height of his powers, training five days a week despite his exile.

So why was he willing to pay such a high price and why did he choose kneeling as a symbolic gesture?

Kaepernick knelt in protest, rather than stand – as is customary – as a polite way of highlighting black deaths caused by police brutality. Such deaths often go unpunished, as black people are treated as second-class citizens, and black bodies as incidental. Earlier that year he'd tweeted how the death of Alton Sterling by two Baton Rouge police officers was 'state sanctioned lynching by means of gun violence'. Similarly, after Latino police officer Jeronimo Yanez shot thirty-two-year-old Philando Castile at a police stop, Kaepernick tweeted: 'A system that perpetually condones the killing of people, without consequence, doesn't need to be revised, it needs to be dismantled!'

At first, during the NFL's 2016 preseason games, Kaepernick sat during the playing of 'The Star-Spangled Banner'; he was inactive, recovering from an injury, and the gesture went largely unnoticed. The backlash began only when he was fully kitted out in his strip and began to kneel before games. Most notably, President Donald Trump, at a rally in Alabama in 2017, encouraged people to counter-protest by leaving the game, and invited NFL team owners to fire whomever 'disrespected the flag', stating that any owner who did so 'would be the most popular person in this country'.

Undeterred, Kaepernick continued to kneel for the rest of the season. Kneeling is not a disrespectful act. We kneel to pray, to propose, to be knighted, in some cultures to eat etc. Former Green Beret and NFL player Nate Boyer actually suggested to Kaepernick that, for this very reason, he should switch from sitting to taking a knee. He gave the example of soldiers paying respect to fallen comrades by taking a knee. For Kaepernick, the gesture was his way of paying homage to the black bodies that had fallen at the hands of the police in America.

In the ultimate irony, it was the knee of a racist police officer that led to the death of George Floyd in Minneapolis in May 2020. No gesture of respect here. Being able to watch his murder on our TVs and phones, evoking the way ancient Roman citizens watched gladiator fights or public executions, changed the narrative. At 8.20 PM, Chicago Avenue in Minneapolis became a global amphitheatre. During a five-minute period, Floyd asked for mercy sixteen times, pleading with the officers that he couldn't breathe. There were three cops on his neck, torso and legs, as one watched. Officer Derek Chauvin never took his knee off Floyd's neck, even when he could see that Floyd was unconscious. The neck restraint manoeuvre is illegal and not permitted by the Minneapolis Police Department. The tactic is known to render its victims unconscious — as forty-four people have been since 2015, by Minneapolis police alone.

How did a routine run to the grocery store turn into a deadly encounter for George Floyd? A white police officer enforced lethal authority by kneeling on his neck for eight minutes and twenty-six seconds, because the culture has decided that 'those people' are to be feared. When I say 'those people', I mean black. But you knew that, right?

Fun fact: Derek Chauvin, the cop who knelt on George Floyd's neck, and Floyd himself share 99.9 per cent of the same genetic makeup. The same is true whatever race you come from. In fact, there is no more genetic difference within a race than there is between races. In *The Chronicle of the Discovery and Conquest of Guinea* (1453), Gomes Eanes de Zurara was the first to describe Africans as a distinct group. Hired by the Portuguese King Henry, he concocted the fallacy of the African as an inferior being. This distinction created the paradigms of blackness and whiteness, which the king used as justification for the Atlantic slave trade pioneered by the Portuguese. Before this bias of an 'inferior people', humans classified themselves according to religion, tribal group or language.

Since that time, the idea of race has continued to be used to justify the brutal exploitation of other human beings for profit. Racism, a tool that has been in effect for over 500 years, is to black people what the coronavirus is to the world as a whole; indiscriminate, the source of attacks without reason and unpredictable, it gives black people the feeling that their lives are on hold as they are forced to navigate it. Racism fundamentally changes the way black people live and move through the world. There is no known cure but, in this case, no group of scientists is working around the clock for a vaccine, Just like a virus, racism mutates with each generation. Often invisible to the eye, systemic racism, like the coronavirus, also needs a host to survive. But, whilst black bodies may fall victim to this virus, black minds and spirits are fed up of living in fear of the bodies hosting this potentially deadly disease. Quite simply, we want our world to stop standing still.

97% Cotton

Laniyuk

'It looks beautiful!' Gawks the sales assistant. I slide my lips into a routine and well performed smile. 'Thank yooooouuuuu,' I mirror back with fake enthusiasm. Holding the loose pleats of the knee-high dress, I gently twist from side to side, mesmerised by its soft cotton sway. It's a delicate summer dress of bright floral print and I look cute as shit. I know it, she knows it, the whole fucking store can see I look amazing.

I slide back into the stall, lock the door behind me and hold my gaze in the reflection of a softly lit mirror, shadows falling down my face. The cut of the fabric slides down my chest, hugs my hips and gently cascades down my thighs. I am mesmerised by me. You could be this kind of girl, I think to myself. You could be a child of summer and sun and flowers and sweetness. You could ride bikes and have picnics. Be delicate on a Sunday and badass on a Monday. You can be both. But in this small chamber, cocooned in this retail conglomerate, I am haunted by ghosts. Echoes of knobbly brown knees, restrained in crisp european dresses, young prisoners to british colonialism's christianity, I cannot unsee the mission in me. These gushing pleats bleed the tears of the parents whose children were ripped from their arms, scratching and prying at the hands of priests. I cannot unsee the mission in me.

As a child, I was quiet and gentle, poised and wide-eyed to my surroundings. I think young me would have loved this dress. But these qualities are not conducive to surviving ongoing invasion. These are not the traits that erected this strong spine, that carved these sharp eyes, that grew this articulate mind. The colony made my softness meek and in this moment I wonder who I might've been. I look into the hardened face of someone I know and yet have never met. A survivor and a resister. A child never allowed to bloom, and I think, once, I knew you.

Standing amongst the faded faces of our Stolen Children, corners singed from disregard, I unzip. Their eyes watch as I remove soft cotton and fold away the tenderness stolen from us. I return the fabric to the arms of the shop assistant and politely shrug. 'Not for you?' she over-empathises. 'No,' I mirror. 'Not quite.'

This Is England. But Not for Me

Nazneen Khan-Østrem

I've never managed to forget this scene in the movie *This is England* (2006). Shaun, a thirteen-year-old skinhead in his new black coat and Doc MARTENS, pops into his local corner shop and brazenly goes up to the owner, Mr Sandhu. He looks at him. Cocky as only a kid can be, he shouts, 'Get me a hundred fags, two bottles of wine, a bottle of whiskey and ten cans of lager. Now!' Mr Sandhu, however, rejects Shaun's dictate. Shaun screams 'Paki' at him and subsequently harasses the shopkeeper. Chaos ensues as Shaun's mentor and friend, Combo, a skinhead seasoned in aggression, enters and waves a massive machete at the terrified owner. They are joined by a couple of other mates who have been spray-painting PAKI on the outside wall of the shop. One of them defecates on the floor while he giggles. In a split second, the corner shop has been vandalised and Mr Sandhu is left in a state of shock.

I know this scene is probably meant to be, in a subtle way, an interlude, a pause in an otherwise bleak story about a working-class community filled with punks, skinheads and outsiders in the Midlands in the 1980s, but it punched me in the stomach the first time I watched it. I've revisited it on numerous occasions, as the movie – written by Shane Meadows – captures a certain sensibility about youth culture and politics, which is rare.

Why is it that this passage in an otherwise brilliant movie continues to haunt me? It is because I could have been one of the kids in the movie, as I used to be a punk — or still am, if I go by the words of the DJ Don Letts: 'Once a punk, always a punk.' I am a Kenyan Asian British Norwegian Muslim female punk. Not a very common thing to be in the 1980s, and not very common now either.

My love affair with punk happened by chance. Having just moved to Norway, I was back in Guildford, where I had spent my childhood, visiting my best friend who had recently embraced the alternative British youth scene. I must have been around twelve. She was fifteen. She played The Sex Pistols and Blondie to me in her bedroom and showed me photos of Nick Cave, then with The Birthday Party. Her hair was long and tussled; she wore a big black ballet skirt and a torn T-shirt, and her eyes were framed by green eyeshadow and black eyeliner. When I look back at her now, she could have played Sean's adorable girlfriend Smelly in *This is England*. I was smitten. I fell in love with the noise, intensity and audacity of the music and the fashion.

I loved Sid Vicious. I dreamed of being Siouxsie Sioux, the lead singer of Siouxsie and The Banshees, and spent hours mimicking her make-up and back-combing my slick black hair, only for it to come tumbling down, despite gallons of hairspray. I adored The Clash and desperately wanted to sing in a band. I bought *New Musical Express* and *Melody Maker*. I read about all the bands, stared at the photos of all the punk idols. Music journalists Paul Morley and Biba Kopf inspired me tremendously with their writing.

But I never saw anyone who resembled me. The journalists were predominately white and male. I visited record stores in London constantly, shy and nervous, flicking through the albums, looking at the bands. On the covers, I saw artists who were obviously from the Caribbean or were white — but no one who looked like they could be of South Asian heritage apart from one obscure band, Alien Kulture, who were emerging from the underbelly of the Rock Against Racism movement in the early 1980s. A sense of loneliness gradually took hold.

Whenever we stayed in London on our frequent holidays – we'd basically moved to Norway physically, but never really mentally – I would walk up and down the King's Road and stare as discreetly as I possibly could at the punks who were hanging around, spitting randomly and drinking their lager. In the early 1980s, I remember striking up a friendship with a Norwegian–British couple on the boat to Newcastle from

Bergen; he was a young British punk who could have been one of the boys on the postcards people used to send from the UK back then – 'Look at these guys!' – with his spiked black-and-red hair.

I would also visit the Great Gear Market, where young designers showcased their latest creations, exhibiting rows of studded shoes or jackets; and Kensington Market where, in the endless rows, I would find like-minded goths who were also into the occult, vampire cults and Hammer House of Horror movies with the irresistible Christopher Lee as Count Dracula. It wasn't easy trying to be a goth when the colour of my skin was golden and nowhere near the pale, transparent look that goths cherished.

I devoured the skinny, scruffy guys with mohawks and ripped jeans, and the girls with their ripped fishnet tights, long black skirts and studded bracelets, a look I tried to adopt — to the total horror of my parents, a prim and proper, Maggie Thatcher-loving couple who dreamed of sending their daughter off to study medicine. That dream, an all-too-familiar straitjacket for South Asian immigrant kids, never seems to fade to grey. But in my world, the cinematic dreamscapes of Derek Jarman made more sense. So did the urban guerrillas in The Angry Brigade and their lure of another lifestyle, or the punks in the anarchist collective Crass, or Poison Girls, or Genesis P-Orridge's industrial sleaze. But I just couldn't see myself there. Where were the Muslim Asian girls? It didn't help that the punks I encountered all too often would talk about 'the fucking Pakis'; I observed as some of them gradually became skinheads fighting for the National Front and, in the process, hijacked a culture that I had to come to believe was inclusive.

Some consolation came through the burgeoning 2-Tone and ska scene, in which Jamaican kids hung out with white, working-class kids from all over and started bands like The Specials. At least there was a scene where people mixed. But the punk movement still felt very white.

When I was fourteen, a ray of hope emerged from the UK indie chart, my guide to all things wonderful: Southern Death Cult, from Bradford. The name of the band, even today, evokes chilling imagery, and it didn't take long before their first single 'Moya/Fatman' was spinning on my turntable. It wasn't Ian Astbury's dark, suggestive singing that appealed to me; it was the fact that the drummer was called Haq Qureishi, a Muslim name of Pakistani heritage. I was fascinated. A punk? Really? I had previously discovered Poly Styrene, over ten years older than me, half-Scottish/Irish and half-Somali, her real name Marianne Joan Elliott-Said. Just the fact that she had a *partly* Muslim surname made me excited. She was the lead singer in X-Ray Spex, one of the most exciting bands of the era. 'Oh Bondage Up Yours!' was released in 1977 and I jumped around in joy. Her unorthodox behaviour inspired me. But I felt closer to the enigmatic-looking Haq Qureishi, who made me start to think that I was not totally alone.

My search for like-minded punk revolutionary souls who were not your classic white kids from Middle England pushed me towards the anarcho-punk band Poison Girls. Vi Subversa was over forty years old and a mum of two when she became the band's lead singer in 1979, and she was Jewish. Poison Girls wrote songs about alienation, fear of freedom, being a real woman (ironically) and tarts. They collaborated closely with Crass, and I dreamed of going to Dial, their self-sustaining farm commune near Epping Forest. But I wasn't sure what my parents would make of my ambitions or if it was a 'decent' thing to do as a Muslim girl.

I was nervous the day I got on the Tube to Walthamstow. Twenty-five years after discovering the revolutionary feminist lyrics of Poison Girls, I had managed to talk Vi Subversa into meeting me. She rarely met journalists, and she'd sounded brusque on the phone when she gave me directions to her house. I wasn't sure what to expect. She opened the door abruptly – hair short, eyes piercing, a ripped T-shirt visible under her apron – and showed me into her lush garden, then vanished. She reappeared after what seemed a lifetime.

At some point, we began an exchange about our religious backgrounds, and she shared her enthusiasm for Jewish anarchists such as Emma Goldman, a heroine of mine. I told her how I missed 'my own'; her face softened as I talked about feeling alienated in the punk movement and about the punks in King's Road shouting 'Paki!' I felt strangely inspired when I left her. Still in awe, I declined her invitation to join her and some others for a vegetarian dinner and instead made my way home across the city, back to south London. I have always regretted saying no. Just as I had felt like an outsider, Vi wasn't exactly surrounded by punk singers in their sixties either. Maybe the idea of being a Muslim punk was just too radical.

A few years later, a new band caught my attention. Fun-Da-Mental's lead singer was Haq Qureishi, now known as Aki Nawaz. Here the political energy from the punk movement had collided with the volatile rhythms of hip-hop; as an extra layer, Fun-Da-Mental had inserted bhangra, strings from Hindi films and unapologetic lyrics about being Muslim and hailing from the Indian sub-continent, quoting the likes of Malcolm X and using imagery from the Iranian Revolution. Their song 'Countryman', released in 1993, brought tears to my eyes; the video showing Aki 'Propa-Gandhi' Nawaz – as he was known then – walking around a village in Pakistan and later experiencing racism in the UK introduced a whole new reality into the British music scene.

For me, it connected directly to what was to become the unforgettable scene in *This is England*. Suddenly, the trials of immigrant workers were highlighted and their heritage celebrated. Nawaz was also one of the founders of the label Nation Records which, from the outset in 1988, was responsible for developing a new dance-music hybrid.

Now I found myself in front of the company's door in All Saints Road, Notting Hill, my heart beating furiously as I waited to meet Aki. I had yet to encounter another person who was both a practising Muslim and a punk and, as an old fan of Southern Death Cult, I was curious to talk to him. I felt an instant connection, despite having a middle-class Kenyan–Asian background and lacking familiarity with Aki's Bradford Pakistani roots.

I would be a faithful fan and a propagandist for Fun-Da-Mental for years to come. This era was filled with hope, and what I would like to see as the true heritage of punk: rebellion and a genuine hybrid culture. Other bands arose at the same time: Asian Dub Foundation, from east London, was another act that embodied the experiences of Muslim families trying to consolidate their roots in the UK. I suddenly felt the solitude of my early punk days fading. And despite them not being Muslim, I was happy when I found Cornershop and The Voodoo Queens, two bands seething with the same ruthless and shameless vigour from the heyday of punk.

I registered both despair and shock when, in 1992, Tjinder Singh, the singer of Cornershop, burnt a photo of Morrissey outside the headquarters of EMI, protesting the fact that The Smiths' lead singer had draped himself in a Union Jack flag during a festival in Finsbury Park. I had been a massive fan of The Smiths, and realising that Morrissey was xenophobic made me incredibly sad. Suddenly a new generation of artists was demanding a voice and, in the process, revealing a dark streak in the punk movement. This brings me back to *This Is England*.

In another pivotal scene in the film, at least in the eyes of this viewer, Shaun and Combo harass three Muslim kids playing football while wearing the traditional shalwar kameez and topis. Combo slides a knife along the cheek of one of the terrified kids. When I watch it now, I wish I could be there with him, so he doesn't have to cry; so I can whisper in his ear that one day his heritage will be celebrated in a manner he can't even imagine.

Years have passed. I can still recall endless gigs with me standing at the front in my leather jacket, probably the only Muslim girl there. I can also remember hundreds of interviews with bands throughout my career as a music journalist where I've felt uncomfortable. But I've always remained adamant about carving out a space of my own, so that others who follow see that we can also be there – in the mosh pit, on stage – making England ours ... so that *This is England* might someday be written in a totally new way.

Alien

Francesca Beard

Host: *the organism in or on which a parasite lives*

You emerge on Earth a human child
Trees rattle ancestral branches
Water otters round your trunk
Light streams colour
Amazement into wonder
You were made for each other

Elytra: *first pair of wings, modified to form a hard shell*

The crash of landing uproots
Who you are, the purpose of your mission
Colonising systems spawn in torn ground
Infesting mother tongues
Bumi Vēr Kē Pokok Alrubbishla
The island runs out of school
You fly to England where water is frigid
Learn to factor words into weapons
You're in deep cover so long
You forget you've never known why

Hyaline: *transparent, like glass*

Skin fair as peeled almond
hair black as blood
east eye slanted west eye round
Which is the rightest?
Your face is open as the moon
common property
a mirror into which strangers stare

Nymph: *sexually immature form usually similar to the adult*

Your dad:
They warned us about the local girls

Men who could be your dad:
Where are you from?
Where are you really from?
You're just like a girl I met in a bar in the war
In Singaporemanilaphuket
So young never guessed she was a pro
This exchange repeats until you accept
It was you in that bar, we are still at war

Cryptic: *colouring and/or pattern adapted for the purpose of protection*

Half-breed you've been gwailo chink-eyed mongrel
    mixed-raced
In and out of so many circles you're fine with BAME
Though you get why anyone who actually belonged
    wouldn't be

Inquiline: *a creature that shares the home of another species without having any obvious effect*

You're a pro
Keep a bag half-packed
At home from home in no one's land
Miscellaneous minority other
Navigating the foreign familiar
Sheltering anonymous under greige umbrellas
You could be anywhere
Not even you know who you are
Where you are going

Girdle: *a strand of silk used to prop up the pupa*

When your daughter ticks the 'white' box
Your hand wrings at your heart
like Olivia de Havilland in *Gone with the Wind*
'But why? I am your mother'
Don't leave me by myself again
You don't say that out loud

Holometabola: *complete transformation*

Your genome migrates to another system
Coded in a body in the body of a craft
Astronauts unlatch; emerge onto pink moss
Release pulsing loops of pheromones
That call response from teeming ghosts
Which form, collapse, coalesce, unswallow
This planet's sky in a breaking wave
Every atomised possible past and future you
Redeems a homing signal of exile and belonging
Abandonment is freedom

The Anatomy of Rejection *OR* The Power of Un-belonging

Raman Mundair

Not quite right for us is a phrase employed in the archetypal editor's rejection letter, a phrase designed to discombobulate. It's a combination of words that are simultaneously encouraging – *you were almost there* – and critical: *Ah, but you didn't cut it, you did not make the grade.* You were the chaff in the wheat, not the cream of the crop. It's a staple cliché that equally condescends and praises; there's a hint of the carrot and a swipe of the stick. The damning, world-weary eye of the editor finds you wanting. You realise that your work, your voice, did not belong in the company of those particular others. Even between the luxurious breadth of pages, you were found to be unamiable bedfellows. You made a *faux pas*. Perhaps you didn't realise? You stick out and do not belong.

Not quite right for us is a challenge, a gauntlet thrown down. Will you take it on? Will you press and query? Will you ask for more detail? Definitions? *Excuse me! What is your version of 'right'? And what is the meaning of this 'quite'? And who, while we're at it, is in fact, 'us'?*

Let's break this down:

- *Quite* – as in *almost, nearly, possibly*, but not. Tantalisingly close.
- *Right* – as opposed to wrong. What is wrong? Anything that isn't perceived as 'the norm'. Right is centred by and rooted in whiteness, patriarchy, being male, straight and able-bodied. This becomes 'the norm'.
- *Us* – is 'the norm' in action. 'The norm' pushes itself front and centre and becomes the default position. Therefore 'us' are the gatekeepers, the guardians of culture and taste. Thus 'us' becomes an established structure, perpetually

growing, rooting its dominant, Western, nationalist and imperial narrative.

Not quite right for us is the schoolyard, where 'us' are picking teams and you're being wilfully ignored. You are overlooked, left for last as the booby prize, your potential untouched, your self-esteem sensitive and raw.

Not quite right for us is the lesbian teen trying to find her place in Queer culture, who cuts her hair short and adapts her style in order to signal: *I am one of you, claim me, let me in*. It's codifying yourself; so you iron out your individuality and complexities in order to be easily read and accepted. It is grieving for a lesbian partner who has died, but her family won't recognise your grief or your lifetime of committed partnership. It is looking for reflections of your lived experience and being told that your experience is niche, unrepresentative of 'the norm'. It is being perceived as deviant and disruptive. It is looking for reflections of you and yours, and never finding them.

Not quite right for us is the 'get right back' foot on the working class. It is fear of the chav, the estate and city academy kid. It's the FARMFOODS/ICELAND versus SAINSBURYS/WAITROSE divide. It's the conservative 'pull-your-socks-up' mantra and the blind belief in a meritocracy that belies the structures of oppression.

Not quite right for us is targeted at a body that doesn't conform, that is abundant and overspills, that refuses to diminish and hold its stomach in. That makes itself obvious by taking up space, that won't smile, act jolly and personable.

Not quite right for us is the disparaging eye that looks at anyone over the age of thirty-five and decides that they have nothing left to give. It is the fetishised obsession with youth. It is Narcissus staring at his own reflection again and again, blind to the life around him, choosing only himself.

Not quite right for us demands an act of shapeshifting in order to gain access to a modicum of power. Priti Patel, Rishi Sunak and Sajid Javid are all interesting examples. It's a crossover from 'them' to 'us' — but at what cost?

Not quite right for us is a prevailing, political, pernicious demonstration of privilege and an assertion of *establishment*. It is this very situation that creates and maintains an inhumane immigration system that places people in limbo, denies human rights and ethical responsibility and implements forced deportations.

Not quite right for us is the upper caste, monied South Asian who has no experience of being without financial stability or privilege within South Asian culture, who can gain traction in Western society and enter at a certain level; typically, a person with education and some social capital behind them. Someone who can approximate a clean version of 'the norm' in action and presentation of values. They move closer to the 'us'. Their version of the 'them' narrative, the dispossessed story, is poignantly pitched. It meets the ears of 'the norm' as a form of harmless entertainment, as manageable multicultural intervention. Tales of wild elephants, kohl-lined eyes, silk saris and the perfect monsoon mango, of exoticised brown bodies moving to a khatak or bharatnatayam beat. Think poised brown bohemian (brahmin or high society Karachi/ Lahori/ Dhaka/ Colombo) writers who offer beautifully crafted, curated versions of the South Asian experience through a privileged lens, or a mediated, soft-focus version of less palatable realities.

Not quite right for us is dog-whistle politics in action, sucking the oxygen out of the room. It is an unquestioning belief in the capitalist system despite its destruction of our planet. It diminishes the opportunity for any dialogue.

Not quite right for us rolls off the tongue, but racism is inherent in the phrase. Take a moment to consider who defines 'right', and what that means. 'Right-ness' – being 'the norm' – is, in the context of race, fundamentally an approximation of whiteness; 'right-ness' is measured in proximity to whiteness. This is where the violence of the phrase is most apparent. It is the one place where, hopefully, you won't be gaslit. The statistics say it all. Surely this reality cannot be denied? It's compounded by the enforced failure of imagination, nurtured from birth, so that young people of colour have to work tenfold to imagine themselves in positions of power, as holders of knowledge, pioneers of science or generally just as successful in life on their own terms.

Not quite right for us is a creative challenge. How, for example, are writers and artists of colour supposed to respond to this? Bend our words and the worlds we create to fit? Dull the rhythms on our tongues? Even then, would the 'us' be able to recognise the value of our art? Would they be able to recognise our genius? Are they equipped? Is it our job to educate them? Even after education, would the nodding gatekeepers have the imagination or experience to know how that translates into lived experience?

How the violence of the phrase, when you have heard it repeatedly, detonates throughout your life. It puts you on an uneven footing. It pushes you way back from the start line. You battle invisible demons. It is a feat to turn up at all, let alone, as the 'us' are fond of saying, 'be in the game to win the game'.

Not quite right for us equals never good enough. It's a placeholder, a 'do not pass go', a reminder of who sets the rules — tacit subjugation. It is a mind game; but perhaps we can choose whether or not to engage and play.

Not quite right for us is an obstacle, an othering, a holding up, a damming of the natural flow. It is a structure that can't simply be adjusted. It must be dismantled. Looking for change in one area of its reach is unlikely to be effective and a waste of time and energy. The intersectional nature of the problem demonstrates that all the issues are important, not just one — and that all, therefore, must be tackled together.

But … *not quite right for us* can also be a threshold. It may be viewed and worked as a liminal space. Despite the hostile conditions we face, we can fashion it into a possibility. It's an opportunity to step back and reflect: *What is the price of being 'us'?* It is a chance to consider closely those who have crossed over, who have become part of 'us'. What have they lost? Is it worth the gain? Is it possible to cross over, and then work to dismantle from within? Or is too much given up in the process of becoming 'us'? What are the strengths in being 'us'? What are the benefits of being distinct?

Yes, *not quite right for us* is the residue, the leftover space that can be transformed. The power of not belonging, the ability to code-switch, to cross physical, psychological, emotional and linguistic borders, alternate tongues, change gear, surprise and shift expectations. It is a moment to step forward and assert our stories louder, to create alternative spaces and platforms for our pioneer voices, at the same time as challenging and gaining access to traditional spaces and platforms. The fact is that there are enough white, male, middle-class, patriarchal, straight and able-bodied voices in the world, enough 'norm'-centred narratives. Now is the time for change, for something else to grow. We can't wait to be chosen, to be let through. We must collectively demand change and, at the same time, forge new pathways. We must see our own value and worth, recognise our own creativity and genius. And we must affirm and choose ourselves.

Biographies

Amina Atiq is a Yemeni–Scouse writer, performance artist, facilitator and activist, awarded the Liverpool John Moore's University Citizenship for her community engagement work. A Young Associate for Curious Minds and BBC Words First Finalist 2019, she has been featured on various artistic platforms including BBC 4 Radio, Arab News, *The Independent*, British Muslim TV and Writing on the Wall. Since the war in Yemen began, Amina has been campaigning with Campaign Against the Arms Trade and Oxfam. Over the last six years she has connected artists and writers directly with Yemeni youth creatives to build a global community. Current work includes being a remote writer in resident with Metal Southend on a new project 'Yemeni Women on the Frontline'.
Twitter: @AminaAtiqPoetry

Francesca Beard is an internationally acclaimed poet and spoken word artist who makes interactive and transformational work, often in collaboration. She's written commissions for institutions such as The Barbican, The Tower of London and The Royal Court Theatre. As a facilitator, she's worked with BBC Radio 3, The Young Vic, B3 Media and All Change to create ambitious, public-facing, participatory shows by and with communities. She has been artist in residence at The Banff Centre, Canada and The Mixed Reality Lab, Nottingham University. Her solo shows, such as *Chinese Whispers*, *How to Survive A Post-Truth Apocalypse* and *Confabulation*, were made in conversation with scientists and researchers, supported by Arts Council England. She comes from Malaysia and lives in London. **www.francescabeard. com**

Sharmilla Beezmohun has worked in publishing since 1994, training at Virago and at Heinemann (African and Caribbean Writers Series). For eleven years she was Deputy Editor of *Wasafiri*, the Magazine of International Contemporary Writing. In 2010 She co-founded Speaking Volumes Live Literature Productions with Sarah Sanders; they were joined by Nick Chapman in 2011. In 2010 Sharmilla's first novel, *Echoes of a Green Land*, was published in translation in

Spain as *Ecos de la tierra verde*. She edited *Continental Shifts, Shifts in Perception: Black Cultures and Identities in Europe* (2016) and, with Sarah White and Roxy Harris, co-edited *A Meeting of the Continents: The International Book Fair of Radical Black and Third World Books* (2005). Sharmilla is a Trustee of Carcanet Publishers, *Modern Poetry in Translation* magazine and the George Padmore Institute, an archive housing unique collections of material from pioneering Black British political and cultural organisations of the last 70 years. She is also on the international organising committee of AfroEurope@s, a cross-continent academic and cultural network.

Jay Bernard is a writer from London and the author of *Surge* (Chatto and Windus, 2019). Jay won the Ted Hughes award 2017 and was named *Sunday Times* Young Writer of the Year 2020.

Maame Blue is a Ghanaian writer splitting her time between Melbourne and London. Her work has appeared in various places including *Black Ballad*, *The Independent*, *AFREADA*, *Storm Cellar Quarterly* (USA), *Memoir Mag* (USA), *Litro Magazine* and *The Good Journal*. Her short story 'Howl' appears in the *New Australian Fiction 2020* anthology, and her debut novel *Bad Love*, published by Jacaranda Books, was longlisted for the Not The Booker Prize 2020.

Paul Burston was born in York and raised in south Wales. His latest novel is the psychological thriller *The Closer I Get* (Orenda Books, 2019). His journalism has appeared in many publications including the *Guardian*, *The Times* and *Time Out*. He is the curator of award-winning literary salon Polari at London's Southbank Centre, and founder of The Polari Book Prize for LGBTQ+ writing. Paul divides his time between London and Hastings.

Michelle Cahill is an Australian writer of Indian origin. Born in Kenya, she has lived in the UK and Australia. Her short stories *Letter to Pessoa* won the New South Wales Premier's Literary Award for New Writing and was shortlisted in the Steele Rudd Queensland Literary Awards. Her honours include the Hilary Mantel International Short Story Prize and *ABR* Elizabeth Jolley Short Story Prize shortlist. She was a Fellow at Kingston Writing School, a Visiting Scholar in Creative Writing at UNC, Charlotte, USA, and a Fellow at Hawthornden

Castle. Her poetry collection *Vishvarupa* has been released as a second edition with UWAP. Her essays have appeared in the *Sydney Review of Books, Southerly, Westerly* and *The Weekend Australian*. She edits *Mascara Literary Review*.

Rishi Dastidar is a fellow of The Complete Works, a consulting editor at *The Rialto* magazine, a member of Malika's Poetry Kitchen, and chair of writer development organisation Spread The Word. A poem from his debut collection *Ticker-tape* was included in *The Forward Book of Poetry 2018*. A pamphlet, *the break of a wave*, was published by Offord Road Books in 2019, and he is also editor of *The Craft: A Guide to Making Poetry Happen in the 21st Century* (Nine Arches Press). His second collection, *Saffron Jack*, is published in the UK by Nine Arches Press.

afshan d'souza-lodhi was born in Dubai and bred in Manchester. She is a writer of plays and poetry, and was recently commissioned to write and direct a short film for Channel 4 (*An Act of Terror*) and a radio play for BBC Sounds (*Chop Chop*). afshan has edited many anthologies and has an essay featured in Picador's collection by Muslim women called *It's Not About The Burqa*. Her debut poetry collection *re: desire* (Burning Eye Books) seeks to investigate the yearning to love, be loved and belong from *desi* (South Asian) perspectives. As well as her own writing, afshan is keen to develop other younger and emerging artists and sits on the boards of Manchester Literature Festival and Pie Radio. afshan also sits on the steering committee for Northern Police Monitoring Project, an independent campaigning and advocacy organisation that challenges police harassment and violence.

Inua Ellams was born in Nigeria. He is a poet, playwright, performer, graphic artist and designer. Inua is the founder of: The Midnight Run (an arts-filled, night-time, urban walking experience.), The Rhythm and Poetry (R.A.P) Party which celebrates poetry and hip hop, and Poetry + Film / Hack (P+F/H) which celebrates poetry and film. Identity, displacement and destiny are recurring themes in his work, in which he tries to mix the old with the new: traditional African oral storytelling with contemporary poetics, paint with pixel, texture with vector. His books are published by flipped eye,

Akashic, Nine Arches, Penned in the Margins, Oberon and Methuen. Inua was specially commissioned to design the cover of this book.

Aminatta Forna is a novelist, memoirist and essayist. Her novels are *The Hired Man*, *The Memory of Love*, *Ancestor Stones* and *Happiness*. In 2002 she published a memoir of her dissident father and Sierra Leone, *The Devil that Danced on the Water*. A book of essays, *The Window Seat*, has just been published by Grove Press (2021). She is the winner of a Windham Campbell Award from Yale University and the Commonwealth Writers' Prize, and has been a finalist for the Neustadt Prize, the Orange Prize, the Samuel Johnson Prize and the IMPAC Award. Aminatta was made OBE in the Queen's 2017 New Year's Honours list. She is Professor of Creative Writing at Bath Spa University and Director of the Lannan Center at Georgetown University.

Gabriel Gbadamosi is an Irish and Nigerian poet, playwright and critic. His London novel *Vauxhall* (Telegram, 2013) won the Tibor Jones Pageturner Prize and Best International Novel at the Sharjah Book Fair. He was the AHRC Creative and Performing Arts Fellow at the Pinter Centre, Goldsmiths in British, European and African performance; a Judith E. Wilson Fellow for creative writing at Cambridge University; and Writer in Residence at the Manchester Royal Exchange Theatre. His plays include *Stop and Search* (Arcola Theatre), *Eshu's Faust* (Jesus College, Cambridge), *Hotel Orpheu* (Schaubühne, Berlin), *Shango* (DNA, Amsterdam) and, for radio, *The Long, Hot Summer of '76* (BBC Radio 3) which won the first Richard Imison Award. He presented BBC Radio 3's flagship arts and ideas programme *Night Waves* and is founding editor of *WritersMosaic*, promoting black, Asian and minority ethnic writers at the Royal Literary Fund. His play *Abolition*, an excerpt from which appears in this volume, will be published in 2021 by flipped eye publishing. **www.gabrielgbadamosi.com**

Richard Georges is a writer of essays, fiction and three collections of poetry. His most recent book, *Epiphaneia* (2019), won the 2020 OCM Bocas Prize for Caribbean Literature, and his first book, *Make Us All Islands* (2017), was shortlisted for the Forward Prize for Best First Collection. He is a recipient of a Fellowship from the Stellenbosch Institute of Advanced Study and has been listed or nominated for several other prizes, including the Hollick Arvon Caribbean Writers Prize, the *Wasafiri* New Writing Prize, and a Pushcart Prize. Richard works in higher education and lives in the British Virgin Islands, where he has just become that nation's first Poet Laureate.

Colin Grant is an author, historian and Associate Fellow at the Centre for Caribbean Studies. His five books include the memoir, *Bageye at the Wheel*, which was shortlisted for the Pen/Ackerley Prize, 2013. As a producer for the BBC, Grant directed several radio drama documentaries including *A Fountain of Tears: The Murder of Federico Garcia Lorca*. He also writes for the *Guardian, TLS* and *New York Review of Books*. Grant's latest book is *Homecoming: Voices of the Windrush Generation*. He became a Fellow of the Royal Society of Literature in 2020.

Xiaolu Guo is a Chinese British novelist, essayist and filmmaker. Her novels include *A Concise Chinese-English Dictionary for Lovers* and *I Am China*. Her memoir *Once Upon A Time In The East* won the National Book Critics Circle Award 2017 and was shortlisted for the Royal Society of Literature Ondaatje Award and Costa Award. Her most recent novel is *A Lover's Discourse,* shortlisted for the Goldsmiths Prize 2020. She was named as a *Granta* Best of Young British Novelist in 2013. Guo also directed several features and documentaries, including *How Is Your Fish Today* (Sundance) and *UFO In Her Eyes* (TIFF). Her feature *She, A Chinese* received the Golden Leopard Award at the 2009 Locarno Film Festival. She had her film retrospective at London's Whitechapel Gallery in 2019 and is currently a visiting professor at Baruch College in New York.

Fergal Harte is a student and freelance writer. He has written over 100 articles for WhatCulture.com on various elements of pop culture, focussing on film, video games and comic books, mediums which he avidly consumes in his spare time. To date his pieces have had over 3.4 million views. After he finishes studying, he aims to pursue a career in screenwriting; well, that is the plan at the moment, anyway.

John Hegley, born 1953, North London, Anglo–French parentage. Schooled Luton and Bristol, graduated Bradford University in the History of Ideas. Honorary Doctorate in Literature, University of

Bedfordshire. John Peel sessions with Popticians,1983/4. Perrier Comedy Award nominee, 1989. Presenter *Word of Mouth* poetry series, Border TV, 1989. *Guardian* Review resident poet,1990-1995. *Pyjama Game* musical 'time study man' principal 1999, Birmingham, Toronto, London. BBC Online poet in residence 2000. Keats House, poet in residence, 2012. Three series, *Hearing with Hegley*, BBC Radio 4. Book titles include *New and Selected Potatoes* (Bloodaxe) and *Glad to wear Glasses* (Carlton). Daughter, Isabella. Partner, Mel. Dwelling, London Borough of Hackney. Football team, Luton.

Kerry Hudson was born in Aberdeen. Her first novel, *Tony Hogan Bought Me an Ice-Cream Float Before He Stole My Ma*, was the winner of the Scottish First Book Award while also being shortlisted for the Southbank Sky Arts Literature Award, *Guardian* First Book Award, Green Carnation Prize, Author's Club First Novel Prize and the Polari First Book Award. Kerry's second novel, *Thirst*, won France's prestigious award for foreign fiction, the Prix Femina Étranger, and was shortlisted for the European Premio Strega in Italy. Her latest book and memoir, *Lowborn*, takes her back to the towns of her childhood as she investigates her own past. It was a BBC Radio 4 Book of the Week, and both a *Guardian* and *Independent* Book of the Year. It was longlisted for the Gordon Burn Prize and Portico Prize and shortlisted in the National Book Token, Books Are My Bag Reader's Awards and the Saltire Scottish Non-Fiction Book of the Year.

Joshua Idehen is a poet, teacher and musician. A British-born Nigerian, his poetry has been published alongside Linton Kwesi Johnson and Anthony Joseph and he has performed at festivals and respected venues across the UK and Europe. He collaborated with Mercury nominated artists The Comet Is Coming and Sons of Kemet, and with dance pop band Benin City on 'Last Night', released in June 2018 by Moshi Moshi Music. He is working on his debut collection and several musical projects.

Andy Jackson has featured at literary events and arts festivals across Australia, in Ireland, India and the USA. His first published book of poems, *Among the Regulars*, was shortlisted for the 2011 Kenneth Slessor Prize for Poetry, and his most recent collection, *Music Our Bodies Can't Hold*, which consists of portrait poems of other people with Marfan Syndrome, was shortlisted for the 2020 John Bray Poetry Award. Andy has co-edited disability-themed issues of the literary journals *Southerly* and *Australian Poetry Journal*, and he works as a creative writing teacher for community organisations and universities. **www.amongtheregulars.com**

Catherine Johnson lives in Hastings, she has written over twenty books for young readers, her most recent are *To Liberty*, published by Bloomsbury, and *Queen of Freedom*, published by Pushkin. Other books include *Freedom* which won the Little Rebels Prize 2019 and was selected as the IBBY Book of the Year in 2020; *Sawbones*, which won the Young Quills prize for Historical fiction; and *The Curious Tale of the Lady Caraboo*, which was nominated for the YA Prize. She also writes for film and television; her work includes *Bullet Boy* and an adaptation of Miranda Kaufman's *The Black Tudors* for Silverprint Pictures.

Linton Kwesi Johnson, an award-winning reggae poet, was born in Jamaica and came to London in 1963. In the 1970s he was in the Black Panthers and worked at the Keskidee Centre, the first home of black theatre and art. Johnson's first poetry collection, *Voices of the Living and the Dead*, came out in 1974. In 2002 he became only the second living poet and the first black poet to have his work included in Penguin's Modern Classics. Johnson's first album, *Dread Beat an' Blood*, was released in 1978; he has since released fourteen more. He is a Trustee of the George Padmore Institute and 198 Contemporary Arts and Learning. In 2020 Johnson won the PEN Pinter Prize.

Tabish Khair was born in 1966 and educated in Gaya, a small town in Bihar, India. He is the author of critically-acclaimed books including the novels *Filming: A Love Story*, *The Thing About Thugs*, *How to Fight Islamist Terror from the Missionary Position*, *Just Another Jihadi Jane*, and the poetry collections *Where Parallel Lines Meet* and *Man of Glass*. His studies include *The Gothic, Postcolonialism and Otherness* and *The New Xenophobia*. Winner of the All India Poetry Prize, his novels have been shortlisted for more than a dozen major prizes, including the Man Asian, the DSC Prize, the Sahitya Academy Award and the Encore. An associate professor at Aarhus University, Denmark, he has been a Leverhulme Guest Professor at Leeds University, UK, and has held fellowships, among others, at Delhi University, Hong Kong City University and Cambridge University.

Nazneen Khan-Østrem was born in Nairobi and is a British Kenyan Asian of Pashtun descent. Raised in the UK and Norway, she has worked as a television presenter for NRK and as an arts and music journalist for Norwegian broadsheet *Aftenposten*. Nazneen graduated from the London School of Economics with a MSc in International Relations in 2000 and started working as an assistant professor in journalism at Oslo Metropolitan University. Her first book, *My Holy War*, about Islam and identity, was published in 2005. In 2007 she was selected for the Edward R. Murrow Exchange Program in Journalism by the US State Department. Nazneen joined Norwegian publisher Aschehoug as a commissioning editor in 2011 and is now a staff commentator with *Aftenposten*. Her book *London: Immigrant City*, written in Norwegian, came out to rave reviews in Norway last year. It will be published in English translation on 1 July 2021 by Robinson.

Laniyuk is a writer and performer of poetry, short memoir and speculative fiction. She contributed to the book *Colouring the Rainbow: Blak, Queer and Trans Perspectives* in 2015, has been published online in Djed Press and the Lifted Brow, as well as in print poetry collections such as UQP's 2019 *Solid Air* and 2020 *Fire Front*. She received Canberra's Noted Writers Festival's 2017 Indigenous Writers Residency, Overland's 2018 Writers Residency and was shortlisted for Overland's 2018 Nakata-Brophy poetry prize. She runs poetry workshops for festivals, moderates panel discussions, and has given guest lectures at ANU and The University of Melbourne. She is currently completing her first collection of work to be published through Magabala Books.

Nick Makoha is a poet and playwright. His debut poetry collection *Kingdom of Gravity* was shortlisted for the Felix Dennis Prize and nominated by the *Guardian* as one of the best books of 2017. Nick is a Cave Canem Graduate Fellow and Complete Works Alumni. He won the 2015 Brunel Prize for African Poetry and the 2016 Derricotte & Eady Prize for his pamphlet *Resurrection Man*. He was the 2019 Writer-in-Residence for The Wordsworth Trust and *Wasafiri* magazine. His play *The Dark* was directed by JMK award-winner

Roy Alexander. His poems have appeared, among others, in *The New York Times*, *Poetry Review*, *Rialto*, *Poetry London*, *Triquarterly Review*, *Boston Review* and *Callaloo*.

Cheryl Martin, co-Artistic Director of Manchester's Black Gold Arts Festival, has worked as a poet, playwright and director. She was a former Associate Director at Contact Theatre and Director-in-Residence at Edinburgh's Traverse. A *Manchester Evening News* Theatre Award winner as both writer (for the musical *Heart and Soul*, Oldham Coliseum Theatre) and director (of *Iron* by Rona Munro, Contact), Cheryl also co-produced and directed an Edinburgh Fringe First winner for the Traverse, entitled *The World Is Too Much*. Cheryl's first solo stage show *Alaska* featured at 2016's A Nation's Theatre, and 2019's Summerhall Edinburgh Fringe and Wellcome Festival of Minds and Bodies in London. Her new solo show *One Woman* won an Unlimited Wellcome Collection Partnership Award; it will premiere in 2021 at Manchester's HOME, going on to a national tour including the Unlimited Festival at the Southbank Centre. Cheryl was part of the 2019-2020 British Council Australia INTERSECT programme. **www.cherylmartin.net**

John Mateer has published books of poems in the UK, Australia, Austria and Portugal. Smaller collections of his work – pamphlets, posters, chapbooks – have also appeared in Indonesia, Macau, Japan and South Africa. His poems have been translated into European and Asian languages and, recently, into Brazilian Portuguese and Armenian. As a 'South African', his poems have been included in *The New Century of South African Poetry* (AD Donker, 2002) and *Imagine Africa*, Vol. 1 (Pirogue Collective, 2011); while, as an 'Australian', his work has appeared in many anthologies in that country. His books in the UK are a small selected poems, *Elsewhere* (Salt Publishing, 2007) and *Unbelievers, or 'The Moor'* and *João* (Shearsman Books, 2013 and 2019).

E. Ethelbert Miller is a writer and literary activist. He is the author of two memoirs and several books of poetry including *The Collected Poems of E. Ethelbert Miller,* a comprehensive collection that represents over forty years of his work. He is host of the weekly WPFW morning radio show *On the Margin with E. Ethelbert Miller* and host and producer of *The Scholars* on UDC-TV. In recent years, Miller has been inducted into the 2015 Washington DC Hall of Fame and awarded the 2016 AWP George Garrett Award for Outstanding Community Service in Literature and the 2016 DC Mayor's Arts Award for Distinguished Honour. In 2018, he was appointed an ambassador for the Authors Guild. Miller's most recent book *If God Invented Baseball* (City Point Press) was awarded the 2019 Literary Award for poetry by the Black Caucus of the American Library Association. **https://searcharchives. library.gwu.edu/repositories/2/resources/367**

Helen Mort is a poet and novelist. She is a five-time winner of the Foyle Young Poets award, received an Eric Gregory Award from The Society of Authors in 2007 and won the Manchester Poetry Prize Young Writer Prize in 2008. Her collection *Division Street* is published by Chatto & Windus and was shortlisted for the Costa Book Awards and the T. S. Eliot Prize. Her second collection *No Map Could Show Them* was shortlisted for the Banff Mountain Literature Award in Canada. She has published two pamphlets with Tall Lighthouse press. Helen's first novel, *Black Car Burning*, was published by Random House in 2019. In 2018 she was elected a Fellow of the Royal Society of Literature. She lectures in creative writing at Manchester Metropolitan University.

Raman Mundair is an Indian-born, Queer, British Asian writer, director, dramaturg, artist and filmmaker based in Shetland and Glasgow. She is the award-winning author of the poetry collections *Lovers, Liars, Conjurers and Thieves* and *A Choreographer's Cartography*, and of a play, *The Algebra of Freedom*. She is also the editor of *Incoming: Some Shetland Voices*. She is a Scottish Book Trust IGNITE fellow. Her short film *Graffiti* is in script development as part of the BFI's Convergence programme. Another short film, *Trowie Buckie*, was shortlisted for Sharp Shorts 2020. Raman is an ALL3Media Scholarship winner and a graduate of the National Film and Television School. She has been invited by the BBC and Screen Scotland's Scottish Drama Writers' Programme 2021 initiative, and is under commission to develop an original drama. She is an intersectional feminist and activist who has worked on a grassroots level against racism, fascism, state violence and gender based domestic and sexual violence, and for freedom of movement within the No Border network. Her work is socially and politically observant, bold, mischievous, cutting-edge, poetic and potent. Her writing plays with the intersections of race, gender, sexuality and class, and challenges notions of British and colonial histories and identities. Raman's work focuses on the lives of people of colour, reframing their experience in a fresh, new perspective. She has performed and exhibited her artwork around the world, from Aberdeen to Zimbabwe.

Ashleigh Nugent has been published in academic journals, poetry anthologies and magazines. His latest work, *Locks*, is a novel based on a true story — the time he spent his seventeenth birthday in a Jamaican detention centre. It won the 2013 Commonword Memoir Competition and has received rave reviews in magazines and online. Ashleigh's one-man show based on *Locks* won support from SLATE/ Eclipse Theatre and Unity Theatre, Liverpool and a bursary from Live Theatre, Newcastle. The show has had very positive audience reviews following showings in theatres and prisons throughout the UK. Ashleigh is also creative director at RiseUp CiC, where he uses his own life experience, writing and freestyle rap performance to support prisoners and inspire change.

Johny Pitts is the curator of the ENAR (European Network Against Racism) award-winning online journal Afropean.com and the author of *Afropean: Notes From Black Europe* (Penguin Random House). Translated into French, German, Italian and Spanish, it won the 2020 Jhalak Prize, the 2020 Bread & Roses Award for Radical Publishing, and is the recipient of the 2021 Leipzig Book Award for European Understanding. He has presented on MTV, BBC and ITV1, and his broadcasting includes a BBC Radio 4 documentary exploring black identity through the music of his father, who was a member of the Northern Soul group The Fantastics. He currently presents *Open Book* for BBC Radio 4 and a forthcoming Afropean podcast funded by a grant from the National Geographic Society. Johny has contributed words and images for the *Guardian*, *The New Statesman*, *The New York Times* and *Condé Nast Traveller*. His debut photographic exhibition *Afropean: Travels in Black Europe* was at Foam in Amsterdam in 2020.

Leone Ross was born in England and grew up in Jamaica. Her first novel, *All the Blood Is Red*, was long-listed for the Orange Prize, and her second, *Orange Laughter*, was chosen as a BBC Radio 4's *Woman's Hour* Watershed Fiction favourite. Her short fiction has been widely anthologised and her 2017 short story collection *Come Let Us Sing Anyway* was nominated for the Edge Hill Short Story Prize, the Jhalak Prize, the Saboteur Awards and the OCM Bocas Prize. The *Guardian* has praised her 'searing empathy' and the *Times Literary Supplement* called her 'a pointilliste, a master of detail…'. Ross has taught creative writing for twenty years, at University College Dublin, Cardiff University and Roehampton University in London. Ross worked as journalist throughout the 1990s. Her third novel, *This One Sky Day*, drops in 2021 with Faber & Faber. She lives in London, but intends to retire near water.

Olive Senior is the prize-winning author of eighteen books of fiction, non-fiction, poetry and children's literature. Her many awards include an honorary doctorate from the University of the West Indies, the Gold Medal of the Institute of Jamaica, Canada's Writers Trust Matt Cohen Award for Lifetime Achievement, the OCM Bocas Prize for Caribbean Literature and the Commonwealth Writers Prize. Her poetry book *Gardening in the Tropics* was on the CAPE syllabus for Caribbean schools and has been translated into several languages, most recently Arabic. She lives in Toronto but returns frequently to her Jamaican birthplace, which remains central to her work. Her book of *Pandemic Poems* which she has been sharing on social media during 'the summer of Covid 19' has just been punlished. Olive Senior is Jamaica's Poet Laureate 2021-24.

Gaele Sobott is a writer based in Sydney, Australia. Her published works include *Colour Me Blue*, a collection of short stories, and *My Longest Round*, a creative biography of boxer Wally Carr. Her most recent short stories appear in literary magazines such as *New Contrast, Meanjin, Prometheus Dreaming, Hecate, Verity La* and the anthology, *Botswana Women Write*. She is founder of Outlandish Arts, a disabled-led arts company. **www.gaelesobott.com**

Jethro Soutar is a writer and a translator. He translates Portuguese and Spanish and has a particular focus on African literature. His translations include novels from Cape Verde, Guinea Bissau and Equatorial Guinea, among them *By Night the Mountain Burns* by Juan Tomás Ávila Laurel, shortlisted for the 2015 *Independent* Foreign Fiction Prize, and short stories from Angola and Mozambique. He is also a founder of Ragpicker Press and an editor at Dedalus Africa. Originally from Sheffield, he now lives in Lisbon.

Shagufta Sharmeen Tania, born in Bangladesh, initially trained as an architect. Her fiction and non-fiction have been published in the Bengali-speaking areas of both Bangladesh and India. To date, she has authored two novels, a compilation of novellas and four short story collections. She also translated Susan Fletcher's Whitbread award-winning novel *Eve Green* from English to Bengali. Her work has appeared in *Wasafiri* ('This Gift of Silver', Issue 84, 2015), *Asia Literary Review* ('Notes from the Ward', Issue 32, 2016) and the *City Press* (issue 7, 2019). Currently, she is working on a novel set during the initial years of war-torn Bangladesh, and a fictionalised biography of a celebrated musicologist of Tagore songs. Shagufta was the recipient of the 2018 Bangla Academy Syed Waliullah Award for her contribution to Bengali Literature.

Jamie Thrasivoulou is an award-winning writer, poet and educator from Derby. His debut collection *The Best Of A Bad Situation* was published via Silhouette Press in 2017. His second collection *Our Man* was published by Burning Eye Books in 2019. He was a winner of the Culture Matters: Bread & Roses Award in 2018, and a 2019 Saboteur Award for Best Spoken Word Performer In The UK. He's the writer-in-residence at HMP Foston Hall and the official poet for Derby County Football Club. The BBC, National Poetry Day and ITV have commissioned his work amongst others.

Selina Tusitala Marsh (ONZM, FRSNZ) is the former Commonwealth Poet, New Zealand Poet Laureate and acclaimed performer and author. In 2019 she was made an Officer of the New Zealand Order of Merit for her services to poetry, literature and the Pacific community. In 2020 Selina was inducted as a Fellow of the Royal Society of New Zealand. An Associate Professor in the English Department at the University of Auckland, Selina teaches Maori and Pacific Literature and Creative Writing. Selina has performed poetry for primary schoolers and presidents (Obama), queers and Queens (HRH Elizabeth II). She has published three critically acclaimed collections of poetry, *Fast Talking PI* (2009), *Dark Sparring* (2013) and *Tightrope* (2017). Her graphic memoir, *Mophead* (2019), won the Margaret Mahy Supreme Book in the 2020 NZ Book Awards for Children and Young Adults and the PANZ Best Book Design for 2020. *Mophead Tu: The Queen's Poem* was published this year.

Byron Vincent is a writer, performer, broadcaster and activist. He has a diagnosis of PTSD and bipolar disorder. He performed for many years as a spoken word artist at music and literary festivals and was picked as one of the BBC poetry season's new talent choices. In more recent years he has turned to theatre, radio and filmmaking, working as a writer, director and performer for the RSC, BAC, BBC and other notable acronyms. Vincent is a passionate social activist with lived experience of issues around poverty and mental health. He has written and presented several documentaries for BBC Radio 4 on the social problems arising out of inequality, ghettoization and mental ill-health. He is currently working on filmmaking and writing a memoir.

Tim Wells is made of reggae, lager top, pie and mash, and Leyton Orient FC. He has been a poet, promoter and historian of all things working class for the past four decades. One of the original 'ranters' of the 1980s, he is the founding editor of the poetry magazine *Rising*. He has worked as a guest poet on Radio London and as writer in residence with Tighten Up, the East London reggae sound system. Recent books include *Keep the Faith* (Blackheath Books, 2013), *Rougher Yet* (Donut Press, 2009), and *Boys' Night Out in the Afternoon* (Donut Press, 2006), which was shortlisted for the Forward Prize for Best First Collection. His first novel, *Moonstomp*, described as 'youth cult meets occult in this New English Library style tale of a skinhead werewolf running riot in late 70s London', was published by Unbound Books in 2019.

Rafeef Ziadah is a Palestinian spoken word artist, academic and human rights activist based in London, UK. Her performance of poems like 'We Teach Life, Sir' and 'Shades of Anger' went viral within days of release. Her live readings offer a moving blend of poetry and music. Since releasing her first album, Rafeef has headlined many performance venues across several countries with powerful readings on war, exile, gender and racism. Rafeef's latest album *Three Generations* offers a moving and powerful remembrance of Palestine, Al-Nakba, exile, defiance and survival. It is a beautiful testament to the human spirit, to 'love and joy against skies of steel'.

Acknowledgements

Warmest thanks go to: Mitch Albert and everyone at flipped eye; Suresh Ariaratnam and his team at Sprung Sultan; Inua Ellams for his book cover design; all the incredible artists – writers, musicians, illustrators, translators – who have been part of the Speaking Volumes journey so far including, of course, the authors in this book; all the wonderful organisations who Speaking Volumes has partnered over the years in the UK and abroad, from festivals to publishers, literature organisations to venues, universities to bookshops; all the behind the scenes arts workers – designers, theatre crews, comms teams, website teams, film crews – for their unstinting hard work which keeps the arts alive; all the funders who have backed us over the last decade, including Arts Council England, the European Union and the Goethe Institute among others. Very special thanks go to Professor Maggi Morehouse, who has been a stalwart supporter of Speaking Volumes over many years, providing us with regular funding contributions that have helped many projects, but also with creative input, support … and laughter. And huge thanks also to Usha Harte for her dedication, and her generous, practical and trustworthy financial advice from the start.

Finally, the greatest thanks must go to my partners in literature, Sarah Sanders and Nick Chapman at Speaking Volumes. What a ride the last decade has been — here's to another one that's as exciting and surprising as it is creatively inspiring.